ACTA UNIVERSITATIS UPSALIE
Studia Anglistica Upsaliensia
77

Reading and Writing Krio

Proceedings of a Workshop Held at the Institute of
Public Administration and Management, University of
Sierra Leone, Freetown, 29—31 January, 1990

Edited by
Eldred D. Jones, Karl I. Sandred, Neville Shrimpton

Uppsala 1992
Distributor
Almqvist & Wiksell International
Stockholm

Printed with the aid of a grant from the Swedish Agency for Research Cooperation with Developing Countries (SAREC).

Abstract

Jones, Eldred D., Sandred, Karl I. and Shrimpton, Neville, 1992, *Reading and Writing Krio*. Proceedings of a Workshop Held at the Institute of Public Administration and Management, University of Sierra Leone, Freetown, 29—31 January, 1990. Acta Universitatis Upsaliensis, *Studia Anglistica Upsaliensia* 77. 73 pp. Uppsala. ISBN 91-554-2868-1

This volume contains eight papers which were delivered at a workshop organised to review some of the practical problems facing readers and writers of Krio, an English-oriented creole language which has its centre in Freetown, Sierra Leone. Besides being the mother tongue of a great number of people, Krio serves as a *lingua franca* throughout the country and forms part of a continuum of related and mutually intelligible anglophone pidgins and creoles extending over large parts of West Africa. Originally only a spoken language, Krio is now increasingly used in the promotion of national development in Sierra Leone. Thus, the papers focus on questions which are of special concern to people working in fields such as health, journalism, broadcasting, drama and education. Among the subjects dealt with at the workshop were questions concerning standardisation, orthography, grammar, the introduction of Krio into the primary school curriculum and translating into Krio. The final article contains a brief report of an ongoing Krio research and publications project funded by SAREC and involving cooperation between researchers at the Universities of Uppsala and Umeå in Sweden and the University of Sierra Leone in Freetown.

Karl Inge Sandred, Department of English, Uppsala University, Box 513, S-751 20 Uppsala, Sweden.

ISBN 91-554-2868-1
ISSN 0562-2719

Printed in Sweden 1992
Textgruppen i Uppsala AB

Contents

Illustrations

A discussion during the workshop at the Institute of Public Administration and Management, University of Sierra Leone (Photograph Sulayman Njie).

Foreword

This volume contains eight papers which were delivered at a workshop organised to review some of the practical problems facing readers and writers of Krio, an English-oriented creole language which has its centre in Freetown, Sierra Leone. Besides being the mother tongue of a great number of people, Krio serves as a *lingua franca* throughout the country and forms part of a continuum of related and mutually intelligible anglophone pidgins and creoles extending over large parts of West Africa. In the last few decades, particularly since Independence, Krio has been very widely used in broadcasting, the theatre, and generally in the promotion of national development in Sierra Leone. There has also been considerable research activity, which has led to the publication of several papers, doctoral theses and a *Krio-English Dictionary*. Moreover, there have been attempts to standardise the orthography of Krio along with the standardisation of the orthographies of other Sierra Leone languages. In the field of education, pilot projects have been initiated to introduce Krio formally into the primary school curriculum.

In collaboration with Dr. Karl I. Sandred, Associate Professor at the University of Uppsala, and Mr. Neville Shrimpton, English Lecturer at the University of Umeå, and with the aid of a grant from SAREC (The Swedish Agency for Research Cooperation with Developing Countries), Professor Eldred Jones organised a workshop to review some of these activities in order to identify residual problems in orthography, grammar, punctuation and capitalisation, and other practical problems facing writers and readers of the language with a view to providing practical suggestions for enhancing the use of Krio as a means of communication.

The workshop was opened on the morning of 29 January 1990 in the Institute of Public Administration and Management, Tower Hill, Freetown, with a speech of welcome by Professor Eldred Jones, who also expressed the participants' gratitude to SAREC which, by its financial support, had made this workshop possible. He saw this and the presence of the Swedish researchers as a sign of how widely Krio was being studied nowadays. Of all the fields in which Krio is being increasingly used in Sierra Leone, he found the great flowering in drama especially noteworthy. He noted that the workshop had been formed by a fairly close group of people working with the language. In the long perspective, however, he wished to see an extension of this work so that eventually an archive of oral Krio literature and folk traditions could be collected to be used as source material for further studies, and he even visualised the establishment of a Krio Research Centre in Freetown.

Ample time was allowed for discussion after every paper. Two papers were read before and one after lunch except on the third day, when the workshop closed after the morning session with a lengthy final discussion chaired by Professor Eldred Jones. Finally, Karl Inge Sandred expressed the participants' thanks to the chief organiser, Professor Eldred Jones, and to Mrs. Marjorie Jones, without whose tireless secretarial work this workshop could never have been held.

The papers published in this volume formed the basis of the discussions, as a result of which a number of practical recommendations were made, including the following:

(a) that the orthography recommended by the Orthographies Workshop of April 1984, with the exception of the symbol ŋ, should be adopted. This would correspond to the orthography already used in the *Krio-English Dictionary*.

(b) that the recommended orthography should be publicised for the benefit of broadcasters, writers and the press, and should form the basis of workshops for various categories of users.

(c) that newscasters who often have to translate important legislation and government statements into Krio should be given their copy in good time to enable them to make accurate translations, and that periodic workshops in the writing and reading of Krio should be arranged for them in collaboration with the broadcasting authority.

The assistance of the following in making the workshop possible is gratefully acknowledged: the Swedish Agency for Research Cooperation with Developing Countries (SAREC) for an enabling grant and for generously funding the printing of these proceedings, the University of Uppsala, the University of Umeå, the University of Sierra Leone, the Institute of Public Administration and Management (IPAM), Sierra Leone, and Mrs. Marjorie Jones, who coordinated the workshop and reproduced the papers. Finally our thanks are due to Professors Mats Rydén, Gunnar Sorelius and Rolf Lundén for including this book in the series *Studia Anglistica Upsaliensia*.

ELDRED D. JONES   KARL I. SANDRED   NEVILLE SHRIMPTON
University of Sierra Leone   University of Uppsala   University of Umeå

Programme

MONDAY 29 JANUARY

9.00 a.m. Opening Statement by Professor Eldred D. Jones
Morning Session, Chairman: Eldred D. Jones
Ajayi Coomber: The New Krio Orthography and Some Unresolved Problems
11.00 a.m. Coffee Break
11.30 a.m. Julius Spencer: Factors Militating against the Easy Reading and
    Writing of Krio in the Theatre
1.00 p.m. Lunch
2.15 p.m. Afternoon Session, Chairman: Gipu Felix George
Raymond E. De-Souza George: Problems Relating to Reading from a Script
    (with Special Reference to Broadcasters, Actors and Other Readers)
3.45 p.m. Discussion

TUESDAY 30 JANUARY

9.00 a.m. Morning Session, Chairman: Alex C. Johnson
Eldred D. Jones: The Business of Translating into Krio
10.30 a.m. Coffee Break
11.00 a.m. Alex C. Johnson: Varieties of Krio and Standard Krio
12.30 p.m. Lunch
2.00 p.m. Afternoon Session, Chairman: Cecil M. Fyle
Eric Johnson: Problems Relating to the Publication of Krio Materials
3.30 p.m. Discussion

WEDNESDAY 31 JANUARY

9.00 a.m. Morning Session, Chairman: Alex C. Johnson
Karl I. Sandred: The Uppsala—Umeå—Freetown Krio Research and Publi-
    cations Project: (1) Introduction
Neville Shrimpton: The Uppsala—Umeå—Freetown Krio Research and
    Publications Project: (2) The Production and Publication of Krio Texts
11.00 a.m. Coffee Break
11.30 a.m. Sulayman Njie: Gambian and Sierra Leonean Krio
12 noon Chairman: Eldred D. Jones
Final Discussion and Closing
1.00 p.m. Lunch
8.30 p.m. Dinner, The Lighthouse Restaurant, Aberdeen

List of Participants

Mr. Dele Charley, Senior Teacher, Services Secondary School

Dr. John Conteh-Morgan, Department of Modern Languages, Fourah Bay College

Mr. Ajayi Coomber, Department of English, Fourah Bay College

Mrs. Gloria Dillsworth, Chief Librarian, Sierra Leone Library Board

Mr. Jonathan Fitzjohn, Lecturer, Milton Margai Teachers' College

Professor Cecil M. Fyle, Director, Institute of African Studies, Fourah Bay College

Mr. Raymond E. De-Souza George, Lecturer, Institute of African Studies, Fourah Bay College

Mr. Gipu Felix George, Director General, Sierra Leone Broadcasting Service

Mrs. Elizabeth Hyde

Professor Alex C. Johnson, Head of Department of English, Fourah Bay College

Mr. Eric Johnson, Ministry of Education

Professor Eldred D. Jones, Emeritus Professor, University of Sierra Leone

Mr. Tim Macauley, Health Education Coordinator

Mr. Donald Mackay, Teacher, Fourah Bay College Preparatory School

Professor Yulissa A. Pat Maddy, Author, Managing Director, Gbakanda Enterprises

Ms. Rosemarie Marke, Ministry of Education

Mr. Sulayman Njie, University of Umeå, Sweden

Mr. Lawrence Quaku-Woode, Author

Professor Karl I. Sandred, Associate Professor, University of Uppsala, Sweden

Mr. Neville Shrimpton, Lecturer, University of Umeå, Sweden

Dr. Julius Spencer, Department of English, Fourah Bay College

AJAYI COOMBER

The New Krio Orthography and Some Unresolved Problems

1. Summary of the Revised Recommendations for the Krio Orthography

At an Orthographies Workshop held in Freetown in April 1984 the participants agreed on a number of recommendations for the spelling of Krio. These can be summarized under eleven points.

1.1   The following letters and combinations of letters are recommended for the Krio alphabet:
a, aw, ay, b, ch, d, e, ɛ, f, g, gb, h, i, j, k, kp, l, m, n, ny, ŋ, o, ɔ, ɔy, p, r, s, sh, t, th, u, v, w, y, z, zh; and corresponding capital letters — (36).

1.2   The name of each letter of the alphabet will be its sound, i.e. phonic articulation will be used.

1.3   Lengthening of a vowel sound will be indicated by doubling the vowel symbol.

1.4   Nasals and nasalization

1.4.1   Nasal vowels are not to be marked by diacritics—the following nasal consonant is enough to signal nasality in the vowel.

1.4.2   Where, within a word, the velar nasal /ŋ/ occurs before a velar consonant, the letter *n* will be used.

1.4.3   In word-final position with variant phonetic shapes the letter *n* will always be used.

1.5   Tone marks should be indicated where necessary: high ´; low `; falling ^; rising ˇ.

1.6   A compound word or reduplication will be written as *one* word.

1.7   Duplications (iterations) will be written as separate words.

1.8   Initiators and terminators, like *o, a*, etc., will be written as separate words.

1.9   Punctuation marks and capitalization will follow the English writing convention.

1.10 Symbols should be incorporated into the orthography for borrowed sounds as necessary, particularly for unassimilated loans.

1.11 The official designation of the language and the name of the people will be *Krio*.

(Extracted from the Summary Report of the Orthographies Workshop held in Freetown, April 24—27, 1984; Ministry of Education, Freetown.)

2. Background

I have given above a summary of the revised recommendations of the April, 1984 workshop; this is for the benefit of those who may not have had the opportunity of reading the report.

The first workshop for the devising of a standardized orthography for Krio was held on the 24th and 25th November, 1981, and certain recommendations were made. Since the standardization of the Krio orthography was part of a project which involved the standardization of orthographies for other indigenous languages, a writers' workshop was conducted in Bo, April 3—9, 1983. Because of its general nature this workshop was more theoretical than practical. I say this because the greater part of the workshop dealt with the presentation of papers on unified systems and harmonization of the orthographies, preparation and production of literacy materials for different levels, etc., and general discussions. However, participants had an opportunity of practising with the new orthographies for Temne, Mende, Limba, and Krio.

During the period January 4—6, 1984, a writers' workshop for the production of materials for Krio primers and the training of teachers was held in Freetown. The materials thus produced were edited and compiled, resulting in the publication of the first two Krio books and their accompanying teachers' guides for use in the pilot primary schools—Book I was a pre-primer, i.e. a reading readiness course, and Book II was the first of two primers to be used after Book I. These books were immediately distributed and put into use in the pilot schools. From our experience in the production of the materials and from feedback from the pilot schools, we felt that it was necessary to have another workshop; and it was this workshop that came up with the revised recommendations given above. However, subsequent training workshops have been held since then, the reports of which have not been published, and Book III has been prepared for publication.

3. Morphophonemic and Phonemic Problems

3.1 *Introduction*

As I have just mentioned, following the April, 1984 workshop, subsequent workshops were held, and some of the areas which may now appear to present problems were discussed and such problems resolved. The April, 1984 summary report itself does not do full justice to the recommendations then made, as it is not explicit enough. It is therefore not surprising that guided by this summary alone one is likely to encounter problems in the use of the orthography.

3.2 *Names of letters* (1.2 above)

According to the 1984 recommendations, phonic articulation should be used in reference to the names of the letters of the alphabet. However, experience in the schools has shown us that, where the children are learning to be literate in English as well, it is somewhat cumbersome and confusing for them to learn the names of the 36 letters of the Krio alphabet by means of phonic articulation. We have therefore decided to retain the English names for the consonant letters (except ŋ), and use phonic articulation for the vowel letters, including diphthongs, and ŋ; a digraph representing a consonant sound should be spelt as two letters. Thus, the Krio alphabet will read as follows:

/a/, /au/, /ai/, /bi/, /si, etʃ/, /di/, /e/ /ɛ/, /ɛf/, /dʒi/, /dʒi, bi/, /etʃ/, /i/, /dʒe/, /ke/, /ke, pi/, /ɛl/, /ɛm/, /ɛn/, /ɛn, wai/, /ŋ/, /o/, /ɔ/, /ɔi/, /pi/, /ar/, /ɛs/, /ɛs, etʃ/, /ti/, /ti, etʃ/, /u/, /vi/, /dɔbulju/, /wai/, /zɛd/, and /zɛd, etʃ/.

And this has proved to be satisfactory.

3.3 *Compounds* (1.6 above)

In the formation of words Krio makes use of blending, that is, two or more words (sometimes the same word, i.e. reduplication) are put together to form one word. And invariably the meaning of the word thus formed (in many cases carrying change of tone) is quite different from the meanings conveyed by the individual words forming its parts. Such a word is written as *one* word, for example:

trángà 'strong' + *yés* 'ears' → *tràngàyés* 'stubborn'
tɔ́n 'turn' + *tɔ́n* 'turn' → *tɔ̀ntɔ́n* 'crooked'
bíg 'big' + *yáy* 'eye' → *bìgyáy* 'greedy'
kér 'carry' + *gó* 'go' + *bríŋ* 'bring' + *kám* 'come' → *kèrgóbrìnkám* 'a gossip'

Thus, we have such contrasts as, for example:

ɔ̀ndàfút 'the sole of the foot' vs. *ɔ́ndà fút* 'under the foot'
tɔ̀ktɔ́k 'loquacious' vs. *tɔ́k tɔ́k* 'persistent talking'
bràwnskín 'a person of fair complexion' vs. *bráwn skín* 'brown skin'
blàkblák 'dark foreign matter often found in local rice' vs. *blák blák* 'intense blackness'
bètbét 'an itching' vs. *bét bét* 'persistent biting'.

In addition to semantic differences, there are cases where the grammatical function of an item also helps to determine whether it should be written as one word or not, as for example:

biguman (adj.) '(of a girl) displaying the traits of an elderly woman' vs. *big uman* (adj. + n.) 'an elderly woman'.

There are also certain words which are single lexical items, despite their repetition of sounds. Such words are written as single words because their parts by themselves are meaningless, for example: *yangeyange, jagajaga, sobosobo, gbaragbara, sambalɛta, ojukokoro*.

3.4 *Duplications* (*Iterations*) (1.7 above)

Successive repetition of words is a common feature of Krio either for emphasis or to express the degree to which a thing is done or said, for example:

kwik 'quickly' vs. *kwik kwik* 'very quickly'
(See also 3.3 above: *tɔk tɔk, blak blak, bet bɛt*). Such words are written as separate words.

3.5 *The intrusive* /r/

A voiced uvular frictionless continuant /r/ (usually referred to as intrusive or linking 'r') occurs in speech between a word ending in /ɛ/, /a/, /ɔ/, or /o/ and the single item *am*. This usage does not extend to words ending in /e/, /i/, or /u/. Therefore it was decided that it should not be represented in writing. It is hoped that readers would have picked it up in their speech before they go on to reading, and so would naturally include it when they read.

3.6 *The suffix* -sɛf *vs.* sɛf

Where *sɛf* is used as a reflexive, it is regarded as a suffix and is therefore attached to the preceding word; but where it means 'even, in fact, also, in addition', it is written as a separate word, for example:

wisɛf 'ourselves' vs. *wi sɛf* 'even we'
di pikin dɛnsɛf 'the children themselves' vs. *di pikin dɛn sɛf* 'the children also'

Thus, we can have, for example, *yusɛf sɛf* 'even you yourself'.

3.7 *Nasals and nasalization* (1.4 above)

3.7.1   Where within a word the velar nasal /ŋ/ occurs before a velar consonant, the letter *n* is used, for example:

/raŋgla/ *rangla*, /ɔŋkul/ *ɔnkul*. Otherwise, the letter *ŋ* is used, for example: *yɔŋbɔy, yɔŋuman*.[1]

3.7.2   A considerable number of words of frequent occurrence in Krio (especially non-content words) show an alternation of variant phonetic shapes in word-final position, conditioned by the initial sound of the following word in connected speech or by a pause boundary.

In such cases, where a nasal occurs before a stop consonant, the nasal is assimilated to the place of articulation of the initial consonant of the following word; thus,

/m/ before bilabial stops,	e.g. /a bim pas/ 'I passed'
/n/ before alveolar stops,	e.g. /a bin tek/ 'I took'
/ŋ/ before velar stops,	e.g. /a biŋ kam/ 'I came'

---

[1] This point was fully discussed in the workshop, and it was recommended that *ng* should be used in all such cases and the phonetic character *ŋ* be abandoned [editors' note].

At a pause boundary or before sounds other than stop consonants, the nasal is elided, leaving the vowel nasalized, for example:

/na fɔ di pikin dɛ̃/ 'It's for the children'
/a bĩ sĩŋ/ 'I sang'
/trɔsis nɔ fayn pã uman/ 'A woman does not look nice in trousers'.

In these cases the orthography provides for the use of the letter *n* always; thus, *bin, dɛn, pan, kin, in, kan*, etc. However, the objective personal pronoun is always written as *am* 'her, him, it'; this is to distinguish it from *an* 'hand' so as to remove possible ambiguity in some contexts, for example:

Dɛn was *an* pan yu (lit. 'They (have) washed (a) *hand* on you') 'You have been cursed'.
Dɛn was *am* pan yu (lit. 'They have washed *it* on you') 'You have been badly cheated'.

3.7.3   Apart from word-final nasals, nasalization of vowels is a regular feature of Krio. Vowel sounds are usually orally produced, but when a vowel occurs before a nasal consonant, it is regularly nasalized in anticipation of the following nasal consonant; in some cases even the nasal consonant is lost, for example:

/fɔmful/	→	/fɔ̃mful/	→	/fɔ̃ful/
/wɛnsde/	→	/wɛ̃nsde/	→	/wɛ̃sde/
/kanvas/	→	/kãnvas/	→	/kãvas/

However, in writing the appropriate nasal letter should always be included in such cases, i.e. *m* or *n*.

3.8   *The emphatic /g/ after /ŋ/*

Sometimes in speech a word which normally ends in the velar nasal, /ŋ/, is given an additional voiced velar stop at the end for the purpose of emphasis, for example: /siŋ/ → /siŋg/, /briŋ/ → /briŋg/. In such a case the letter *g* should be added in writing and the nasal represented by the letter *n* (see 3.7.1 above); thus /siŋg/ *sing*, /briŋg/ *bring*.

ALEX C. JOHNSON
Varieties of Krio and Standard Krio

1. Introduction

A variety is the technical term for a type of language identified by linguistic features on several levels which distinguish it from other types.[1] The notion of variety is crucial for the study of language variation, and language variation has been a pre-occupation of sociolinguists, creolists, researchers into world varieties of English and all interested in the responsiveness of language to social, demographic and geographical realities.[2] This paper examines the synchronic state of Krio from this perspective.

The notion of variety is not here coterminous with dialect as the term "dialect" would be inappropriate since it more accurately refers to varieties according to region and geographical location of users.[3] In the case of Krio, this would account for only one aspect of a very complex situation.

Thus, there are varieties of the Krio language, and what we normally refer to as "Krio" is both the common core and the different variety realizations spoken around us. The varieties discussed below share a set of grammatical, phonological, lexical and contextual characteristics that constitute this common core on which the question of a standard turns.

A standard can be identified only for the written language in orthographic representation, grammar and vocabulary, but since Krio has only an incipient written tradition, the problem becomes difficult of resolution as the primacy of the spoken word exacerbates variation. The standardizing impact of the *Krio-English Dictionary*[4] seems lost on our non-specialist writers and there is the need to promote a standard variety.

---

[1] This definition is after the neo-Firthians. Another expression of the notion in socio-linguistic terms occurs in Hudson, R.A., 1980, *Sociolinguistics*, Cambridge, p. 24: "What makes one variety of language different from another is the linguistic items that it includes, so we may define a variety of language as a set of linguistic items with similar social distribution".

[2] Pidgin and creole linguistics and the socio-linguistics of world varieties of English have produced a large number of books and journals in this area. See Jones, E.M.K., 1985, *Dialect and Other Varieties of Sierra Leone Krio*, a dissertation submitted for the degree of M.A. in English at Fourah Bay College, University of Sierra Leone, Freetown.

[3] Other possible varieties are registers and stylistic variants, both not within the ambit of this paper.

[4] Fyle, C.N. and Jones, E.D., 1980, *A Krio-English Dictionary*, Oxford and Freetown: Oxford University Press and Sierra Leone University Press.

In isolating varieties, each is marked by sets of indexical linguistic features of phonology, grammar and vocabulary.[5] A convergence of these levels is preferred though a variety can be realized predominantly on one level. Notwithstanding this, for a variety to have a conclusive mode of existence and be considered seriously in the quest for a standard, a significant convergence of levels is essential.

2. Dimensions of Variety Differentiation

The often discussed dimensions of variation in Krio are the geographical (village, town, provincial, Fourah Bay), the temporal (age distinctions), the social class, and in terms of the mode of acquisition of the language.

2.1. *The Geographical*

Loosely interpreted, this can be said to relate to the demographic fact that the approximately 2 % or 50,119 (1974), 64,403 (1985) of the Sierra Leone population who are native speakers of Krio live almost entirely in the Western Area.[6] These Krio speakers have the social and temporal variants, and other usually attested types such as 'village', 'deep' and 'Aku' Krio.[7] They could be considered as the users of the K_1 or native-speaker variant.

But the Western Area is host also to many Krio-speaking Sierra Leoneans with other Sierra Leonean languages as L_1 some of whom also, in infancy and childhood, have acquired Krio like native speakers alongside these languages.[8] In addition, there are others who, though non-Krio in ethnic origins, because of their Western Area and/or westernized socialization experience, control only English and Krio.[9] Other patterns of social behaviour are displayed by non-Krio Western Area indigenes who interact in the home, work, neighbourhood and other domains entirely in Krio.

---

[5] Gregory, M., 1967, "Aspects of Varieties Differentiation", *Journal of Linguistics* 3, 177—198.

[6] Native Krio speakers were approx. 1.9 % or 50,119 of the Sierra Leone population in the 1974 census. The same percentage when applied to the 1985 census would give some 64,403 native speakers. See Johnson, A.C., 1985, "National Language Policy and the Sierra Leonean Languages in Education", *West African Languages in Education*, ed. Williamson, K., Vienna, 55—79, and Johnson, A.C., 1989, *The Role of the Languages of Minority Groups as Languages of Instruction and Vectors of Culture. Case Study of Sierra Leone*, UNESCO NIEDA Paris/Dakar.

[7] The Aku Krios are Moslems concentrated at Fourah Bay in the east end of Freetown and said to control a distinctive variant.

[8] Diebold, A.R., 1961, "Incipient Bilingualism", *Language* 37: 97—112 describes this as "childhood acquisition of two or more native languages".

[9] Due to social change this class of Krio users is growing.

For some of these groups, either the K_1 variety or the K_2, modified in phonetically and grammatically acceptable ways, could be considered their geographical variant. Thus in the first and third groups, this approximation of the K_1 variety varies with the length and degree of exposure to Krio, their educational and social background and, inevitably, the strength of native language interference. In the second group, there is the odd but not unusual situation of those born overseas and now domiciled in this area and those born locally but who somehow never acquired their parents' native languages, all having only English and Krio. This when coupled with their social and educational background means a competence that is native-like.

We therefore find in the Western Area not one geographical "dialect" but a complex variety continuum among non-native speakers ranging from the most acrolectal, i.e. similar to and even identical with the native-speaker's K_1, through the mesolects to the basilectal which is removed from, less close to the K_1, more L_1-influenced and untypical of the native speaker. Native speakers also show an acrolect–basilect contrast as will be presented later.[10]

Outside the Western Area, the provincial non-native users of Krio represent some two-thirds of the population and for them it is a *lingua franca*, technically a pidgin or contact language and their second, third, fourth language.[11] This is a multilingual geographical setting with the interference phenomenon being the crucial factor. Correlating setting and variant presents us with the usually attested K_2 or non-native variety, which is predominantly mesolectal and basilectal in terms of the K_1, as it contains those features of the L_1 which have different degrees of acceptability. The complexity of Krio variety differentiation on this dimension is therefore obvious.

2.2. *Acquisition Pattern*

Given the multilingual setting of Sierra Leone and the use of Krio as the national *lingua franca*, the conditions under which Krio is acquired are relevant to variety differentiation. The parallel acquisition of Krio and other Sierra Leonean languages in the Western Area and its acquisition alongside or after

---

[10] The terms acrolect, mesolect and basilect are used here with reference to the extent to which a variety approximates to the most prestigious normative type where a continuum may be said to exist; in this case the acro-, meso- and basilect are stated in order of decreasing degree of prestigiousness. Hence for K_1 the acrolect is the social class variant which tends towards English and the basilect the mainstream variant. For K_2 speech, the acrolect is the variant which approximates to that of the native-speaker, *not* English. The mesolect represents shades between this acrolect and the basilect, the latter being the variant furthest removed from the native-speaker norm.

[11] See Johnson A.C. 1985 and 1989 for estimates of the proportion of the Sierra Leone population who use Krio. Cf. note 6 above.

English is such a reality of socialization in this setting that the distinction between native K_1 and non-native K_2 in the identification of varieties has to be approached with care. It is also clear however that where Krio is learnt as a second or third language and interference features are not refined out, the ensuing variety will necessarily be quite unlike the native speaker's.

2.3. *The Temporal*

This dimension relates to the putative variety differentiation according to age and is a distinction exclusive to native speakers. The older generation of Krio speakers, variously 60 + or 70 +, and who are usually, though not exclusively, largely found in the villages, are associated with features not found among young people. The question is whether these are enough, convergent and with a high degree of occurrence to allow a discrete and attestable type.

2.4. *The Social "Class" Dimension*

On this dimension, the main determining factors are educational background, social standing and exposure to English and, to some extent, wealth. These point to an incipient decreolizing situation. The Krio aristocratic class and intelligentsia of the colonial era may have now been diluted, eclipsed and largely neutralized with continued social change, but their tendencies survive in the linguistic behaviour of the new "middle class" who with education, continued exposure to English, use of English in informal domains, and a readiness to allow code-mixing and interference show attitudes that are at once linguistic and sociolinguistic. This tendency is now institutionalized and appears to be spread both vertically and horizontally with education, and the variety is realized in the features discussed below.

These dimensions of variation, individually and when they intersect or converge, condition the attested varieties in modern Krio. There is however the question of whether each variant does exist. Is there conclusive linguistic evidence in the form of overt indexical linguistic features and their frequency of occurrence in current usage among the groups controlling such varieties?

3. Indexical Linguistic Features of Varieties

The Krio native speaker's variant has the common core features of grammar, vocabulary and phonology from which all others can be shown to diverge. The *Krio-English Dictionary* provides a reference point for the lexicon; native speaker intuition is the yardstick for the grammar in judging what is grammatically acceptable in the absence of a published grammar or dictionary of usage. For phonology, the phonemes can be represented orthographically as follows:

Vowels:	i	e	ɛ	a	ɔ	o	u	
Diphthongs:	ay	aw	ɔy					
Consonants:	p	b	t	d	k	g	kp	gb	m
	n	ng	ny	j	ch	f	v	th	s
	z	sh	zh	h	r	l	w	y	

There are seven pure vowels or monophthongs, three diphthongs and twenty-six consonant sounds represented here, and there are nasal counterparts to the oral vowels. This phonology includes the suprasegmentals of tone and length not represented here orthographically, and syllable structure is $(C_{0-3}) V(C_{0-3})$. It is the phonetic realizations (in their normal distribution) of the sounds represented here which make the native Krio speaker sound as he does when using his lexis and structure. These grammatical, lexical and phonological items are those found in the mainstream native-speaker variety, the K_1.

Now there is evidence that the K_1 native-speaker continuum involves divergence and variation along the acrolectal and basilectal planes in response to the conditioning factors discussed in sections 2.1, 2.3 and 2.4 with respect to the Western Area and the temporal and social "class" dimensions.

3.1. Thus, in the village settings, due to differences in the environments, in social and economic experience and activities and the uneven degree and type of language change, there are identifiable features in the speech of, in particular, the older generation. Specialized lexical items such as *takute* 'a trap' and *okele* 'a helping of foofoo'; the vowels *a* for *o* in *shala* as against *shalo* 'shallow' or *a* for *i* in *tanap* in contrast to *tinap* 'stand up'; the consonant *s* instead of *sh* in *fis* 'fish' and the removal of the cluster in *ton* as opposed to *ston* 'stone' are a few examples. It is however difficult to accept that these have a high incidence and frequency of occurrence in current village usage only.

3.2. On the temporal plane, older users are usually associated with archaisms, some distinctive phonetic features and vocabulary, a striving for pure or "deep" Krio, characteristics which are absent from the speech of young users, who are normally seen to control a mainstream K_1 type. In phonology we have *ɛ* for *e* in *snek*, *a* for *i* in *tanap* and the lost *st* cluster in *ton os* 'stone house', palatalization of *g* and *k* in *gyal* 'girl' and *kyanwud* 'camwood' and some other features also found in village settings. Research has not yielded significant grammatical features but numerous vocabulary items can be assembled: *miniral, ospikin, ɔmɔle, abana, biba, nikaz, shimi, bedshɔ, sɛnjago, jɔmbul, jokaki, swank, tay ɔja, kekɛnwayn.*

A close scrutiny of these items would reveal that some have indeed been displaced by new terms even among older people, viz. *sɔft* (*miniral*), *pants* and *slip* (*nikaz* and *shimi*), *prɔs* (*sɛnjago*), *blɔf* (*swank*); some are in free variation with newer terms among the old and even in the speech of young people, viz. *ospikin* and *ɔmɔle, nikaz* and *pants, swank* and *blɔf*; others have lost their referents and therefore been displaced, such as *jɔmbul, jokaki*, and *tay ɔja*, now *tawa*, and *kekɛnwayn*, now *risɛpshɔn*. Though some features continue to be marginalized, e.g. the phonetic, there will continue to be a variant based on age, especially on the level of the lexicon. But while there are these distinguishing indexical features the common core persists.

3.3. More readily identified is the sociolect which represents an early stage of decreolization.[12] The variety is marked on a number of levels—the phonological, the lexical, the grammatical and by code-mixing—which converge to make it the most significantly foregrounded and current type.

Phonology: In this variety we have, *thik, bath, wɔsh, ticha, kandul, gal*, for *tik* 'thick', *baf* 'bath', *was* 'wash', *chicha* 'teacher', *kyandul* 'candle', *gyal* 'girl', respectively, which show consonant choice.

For vowels we note, *ɛg, yɛlo, wɔsh, wɔta, sɔn, tikɛt, makɛt, flɔ, wɔk, wia, dawn, tawn, nayt, rays, haws* for *ɛg* 'egg', *yala* 'yellow', *was* 'wash', *wata* 'water', *san* 'sun', *tikit* 'ticket', *makit* 'market', *flo* 'floor', *wok* 'work', *wɛr* 'wear', *dɔng* 'down', *tɔng* 'town', *nɛt* 'night', *rɛs* 'rice', *os* 'house'—all with various kinds of vowel substitution.

Cluster simplification or reversal can be seen in *ask, dɛsk, ɛskep* instead of *aks* 'ask', *dɛks* 'desk' and *ɛkskep* 'escape'. On the suprasegmental level, this variety shows a tendency to use stress patterns on African names and on English-derived names instead of the tonal patterns which normally accompany assimilation e.g. *'Sise, Ko'roma, 'Alis*, rather than *Sìsé, Kòròmá, Àlís*, i.e. Sesay, Koroma and Alice.

---

[12] Decreolization is the gradual process by which a creole language merges with the corresponding and antecedent standard language to which it is exposed in the same speech community. It could lead to a post-creole continuum situation as in Jamaica or even complete the cycle back to English as with Black English in the United States.

Grammatical features include code-mixing and using words, expressions and structures from English or which are English-coloured in preference to the mainstream forms.

1. *a dɔn tɛl yu se ay kant ɛlp it*
   I have told you that I can't help it
2. *a dɔn tɛl yu se natin nɔ de we a kin du*
   I have told you that there is nothing I can do
3. *a sɔspɛkt so*
   I suspect so
4. *a tink so*
   I think so
   a want fɔ fil so
   I want to feel so
5. *mɔs sɛn di mesnaz kam*
   Do send the masons
6. *kɔm to think ɔf it*
   Come to think of it
7. *bɔys kwɔtaz*
   Boys' quarters
8. *ay dont think so*
   I don't think so
9. *di hawzis ɛn kaz we i gɛt*
   The houses and cars which he has

Examples 1, 3 to 9 have alternatives in mainstream usage; thus 2 is mainstream and less acrolectal than 1, as is the first item in 4, which could replace 3 as well as the second item in 4.

On the level of vocabulary, the following are examples of numerous attested items, and for this variety every English word is a potential Krio word: *mit, ips, brɛst, Krismas, bath, spring ɔnyɔns* for *bif* 'beef/meat', *wes* 'bottom', *bɔbi* 'breast', *baf* 'bath', *lif yabas* 'leaf onions'.

These levels mark this variety as the most acrolectal of the native-speaker variants, especially when one considers the ease with which English vocabulary and expressions are incorporated without significant assimilation. In contrast to it is the mainstream basilect which the non-native speakers in the Western Area approximate to or diverge from in varying degrees in the non-native lectal continua. This basilect is also that which the temporal (age) and geographical (village) types diverge from in ways already discussed.

3.4. The non-native K_2 variety does not, on the phonological level, make use of all the K_1 phonemic segments identified above, even where some are found in the users' native languages. All the Krio vowels occur in the other Sierra Leonean languages with Temne having two more vowels. The consonants in the five Sierra Leonean languages used here differ from the mainstream K_1 type in that the following are absent:

Mende:	ch, j, th, sh, zh, z, r.
Temne:	g, kp, ch, j, ny, sh, zh, v, z.
Limba:	g, kp, gb, ch, j, ny, sh, zh, v, z.
Kono:	g, j, th, sh, v, z, r.
Fula:	kp, gb, ch, j, ny, sh, zh, v, z.

Their syllable structure also differs since it is the basic CVCV type. These segmental and syllabic features apart, the distribution of phonemes and treatment of clusters are important in producing those characteristic phonetic features which are distinctively K_2.

Phonology (K_2 items are on the left in each pair).

Consonants:	*tɛk—chɛk, tɔt—chɔch, yomp—jomp, yam—jam, sip—zip, bim—vim, sɛbim—sɛvin, bilif—biliv, suga—shuga, masin—mashin, mɛyɔmɛnt—mɛzhɔmɛnt*
Clusters:	*situl—stul, kɔshɔn—kwɛstyon, tiret—tret, piles—ples, sipun—spun, mindul—midul, bɛlɛful—bɛlful*
Syllable structure:	*wuna—una, ifi—if, wopin—opin, bɛlɛful—bɛlful, sitɛp—stɛp*
Vowels:	*ɔrɛt—ɔrayt, wɛl—ɔyl, wut—wit, wot—wet*

One observes substitution of vowel and consonant segments due to interference, the splitting of clusters to conform to the CVCV syllable structure and the closing of initial open syllables for similar reasons.

Grammar presents areas of divergence though not as extensively as phonology.

i. K_2 adds sentence tags like *so, ba, ɛ*:
    na in so—It's him—*na im*
    ɛ na so i tan—It's like that—*na so i tan*
    na wetin ba—What is it—*na wetin*

ii.   Word order and co-occurrence features:
    i de kam wit rɔn—i de rɔn kam
    He approaches running
    i nɔ want; mi i nɔ want—a nɔ want
    I don't want (it)
    pas fɔmi da pan—pas mi da pan
    Hand me that container

iii. Lexico-semantic shift:
wetin yu sɛn fɔ mi—wetin yu bring fɔ mi
What have you brought for me?
mi ɛn yu—wi [ɔltu] ɛn yu
Me and you/You and I

iv. Prepositions:
i de pan wok—i de wok
He is working
a lɛf am pan bruk—a lɛf am de bruk
I left him laundering
I kam wit rɔn—I rɔn kam
He came running
na mi padi wit am—na mi padi
He is my friend

v. Split serial verbs:
i de go ɛn rɔn—i de rɔn go
He is running and moving away

The lexicon does present some typical items as well as lexico-semantic divergences which mark the type. These features of the K_2 variety depend for their incidence in the speech of individuals on variable conditioning factors including socio-educational background, use and exposure to English, acquisition and socialization patterns and degree of exposure to Krio. Thus, though the potential for variety differentiation here is enormous, the actual variety which the above examples represent could be heard in the speech of some of the K_2 characters in "The Professionals".[13] The degree of incidence of these features in other K_2 users attests to the lectal continuum here as well.

4. A Standard Krio Variety

Variation will continue in Krio due to the continued existence of the conditioning factors and because languages exist in social settings which promote it. The relevant consideration therefore is which varieties would be enhanced, levelled out or become dominant, and also which variant has claims to being the standard.

---

[13] "The Professionals" is a popular comedy group which among other things exploits variety differences for comic effects.

The mainstream K_1 variety seems set to gain dominance over those associated with the geographical (village vs. town) and temporal (age) dimensions. The latter will continue as people are dispersed and located in various places, and also grow old with consequent changes in the settings within which they use the language. But with better communications, education and mobility, with their attendant standardizing influences, these less marked types seem likely to be marginalized as the mainstream becomes more and more the norm.

The social variant of the K_1 appears to be spreading outwards and downwards, especially in its phonology and vocabulary. Items like *bath, pakɔ, bɔys, kwɔtaz,* etc. have replaced the basilectal *baf* and *kpakɔ,* and *kwɔtaz* and *kwataz* are in free variation, and code-mixing and adoption of English lexicon are important features of this variety. Its future and that of the mainstream will depend on whether the sociolinguistic conditions making for the impetus towards decreolization continue to exist.

At its simplest, a standard is usually the variety which is most intelligible and acceptable to native speakers and to the wider speech community, the most dominant and the one which calls least attention to itself over the widest range of usage. It is also the norm for writing and usage. Of the variants discussed above, the mainstream K_1, rather than the acrolectal K_1, would appear to have claims to standard Krio status and should be promoted as such.

Since a standard written language is compatible with variation in educated accents, standard Krio, in the natural run of things, would be spoken with the native speaker's and other more acceptable non-native accents. The uneducated accents, with intrusive, stigmatizing interference features, would be recognized for what they are by the speech community. It is hoped that the development of a written tradition will promote the standard whatever the accents associated with it.

ELDRED D. JONES
The Business of Translating into Krio

For most of its history, Krio has been a language confined almost exclusively to oral communication, although there have been fitful attempts to write it ever since the middle of the nineteenth century. I have made reference to some of these attempts in my articles "Mid-Nineteenth Century Evidences of a Sierra Leone Patois" and "Krio in Sierra Leone Journalism".[1] The language has been very effective as a domestic medium of communication and adequately covers all aspects of ordinary life: family relationships within Krio society, cooking, institutions surrounding birth, death, marriage and other social customs. It is also the language of the market place—the language of the 'an-to-mɔt' sector of the society (to borrow a very recent effective coinage). It has finally become established as the *lingua franca* which unites the various language groups of Sierra Leone and is the language of address on inter-tribal occasions. It is increasingly used in religious worship and *The New Testament* has recently been translated into it. The national news, legislation and public notices are regularly passed on by radio through Krio translations to the public. During the last twenty years or so, the language has been used over a much wider area than the domestic or 'an-to-mɔt' sectors. It is being required to express objects, concepts and ideas it had never been called upon to cover in the greater part of its existence. The business of translating into Krio has therefore assumed an urgent importance.

Thomas Decker, from the 1930s until his death, was aware of the need to use Krio much more widely than it had been previously used and he sought to prove that it was capable of such wider usage. It was his conviction that Krio could be used to express almost anything that could be expressed in another language and he sought to prove it by making translations from two of the most important landmarks of English Literature—the authorized version of *The Bible* and the works of William Shakespeare. In his introduction to his adaptation of Shakespeare's *As You Like It* (*Udat Di Kiap Fit*), he had written as follows about his earlier translation of *Julius Caesar* and his new adaptation:

Acknowledgement: This article was written with valuable assitance from Mrs. Marjorie Jones.

[1] *Sierra Leone Language Review* 1 (1962) and 3 (1964).

Thomas Decker, OBE (1916—1978), Krio author and ardent champion of the Krio language.

In that exercise my aim was twofold: first, to make propaganda for the Krio language by proving that the most serious things can be written and spoken in it and secondly, to make it possible for people who had not had the opportunity of reading Shakespeare at school, to taste of the excellence of this great writer by seeing one of his most popular plays staged in their own language. Consequently my translation of *Julius Caesar* was almost word for word. In the present exercise my main aim is to amuse and I have therefore refrained from any slavish translation and indulged in bold adaptation.[2]

Thomas Decker remained the most ardent propagandist for Krio until his death, and his versions of *Julius Caesar* and *As You Like It*, as well as other selections from Shakespeare and some from *The Bible* are among the best translations into Krio that we have to date.

It is worth noting that although he adapts *As You Like It*, changing the title, the names of the characters, the location and the flora and fauna—making all these tropical and specifically Sierra Leonean—yet he follows Shakespeare's text otherwise very faithfully and his translation is often quite felicitous. I shall return to his translation later. What Decker foresaw and anticipated has now become a reality. It is now an urgent necessity for Krio to be used to translate the "most serious things" that Thomas Decker had foreseen, and because there has not been that much practice in the art of translation and because even Thomas Decker's own translations are not that widely known and studied, translators have had to work in a hurry and almost in the dark. Newsreaders are often confronted at short notice with Government legislation which they have to translate on the air looking at the English text. They have to cope with complicated syntactical forms, fine distinctions of meaning and strange technical terms. Their efforts often demonstrate the need for the business of translation to be treated far more professionally than it is at present.

A very significant recent development in this area is the translation of *The New Testament* into Krio.[3] The translation of *The Bible* under the patronage of King James—the authorised version—had and continues to have a very great influence on the English language. Thus, if it is widely used, the Krio version of *The New Testament* should have a similar effect on the language; it is important therefore that that text should be very closely studied and when necessary revised so that a standard version could be produced. Work is under way to translate parts of *The Book of Common Prayer* into Krio and if this is done and successfully used, it would also have a significant influence on the development of the language. One other area in which the potential of Krio is being very actively exploited is that of commercial advertising on the radio.

---

[2] *Udat Di Kiap Fit* and Decker's *Julius Caesar* exist in unpublished mineograph form as well as in the Umeå University *Krio Publications Series*.

[3] *Gud Yus Fɔ Ɔlman, Di Nyu Testament*, Copyright United Bible Societies, 1987.

Some advertisers use only Krio in their commercials while others use both English and Krio to advertise the same products. It is an interesting exercise to see how copy-writers translate from one language into the other.

All these new uses are stretching the resources of the language and it is necessary to pause and see some of the problems involved in translating into Krio. First of all, why is it necessary at all to translate into Krio? The answer is obviously because it is the language that most people understand. Since English is learned mostly in school and goes with literacy in a population where no more than some ten to fifteen per cent are literate, it is vital to pass on information in a language which most of the population can understand. A small percentage of the people who listen to Krio can speak English as well, having been educated in that language. For most of these the Krio translation is superfluous and sometimes even a source of amusement; but for the less well educated among them it may still be of some use. It is however the main source of information for the vast majority of the urban population; for them it is no luxury; it is something of vital importance, particularly at a time when for various reasons public notices sometimes never get printed at all and are only conveyed through the radio. It is therefore most important that what is rendered in Krio is accurate and as elegant as possible.

Anyone who has attempted translations from English into Krio must be aware of some of the problems which are very soon encountered. The most obvious difficulties arise from the vocabulary. The vocabulary of Krio, for most of its history, as I have indicated before, has been confined to the domestic and the 'an-to-mɔt' sector. It is perfectly capable of coping within those areas. It has not been used, for example, to express scientific concepts, political ideas or to cope with the subtleties of legislation and so on. It has also been a very practical language, tied to the concrete rather than the abstract; it has therefore not been very much used to express abstract ideas and is short of words indicating concepts rather than objects. The easiest way out of problems of vocabulary is borrowing. But if we take into consideration the fact that the object of the translation is to communicate to people who have never been to school, then the effort of translation is rendered useless if terms are imported wholesale from one language into the other. Where no terms exist in Krio the translator would have to adapt, to stretch existing words, or to employ periphrasis or explanation in order to convey the ideas in his original. This is itself a delicate business since in the process of explanation, slants and subjective interpretations may be introduced. The task of the translator is to digest the material and reproduce it in intelligible and idiomatic Krio, and this, I suggest, cannot be done with a difficult piece of English on the spur of the moment.

Let us look at Thomas Decker's practice. He is after all, our greatest translator to date. Even before he translated *Julius Caesar* he had produced

UPPSALA UNIVERSITET
Engelska institutionen
UNIVERSITY OF UPPSALA
Department of English

6.5.1992

Professor Elizabeth Tonkin

Department of Anthropology
Queen's University
Belfast BT7 1NN
Northern Ireland

Dear Elizabeth,

　　At long last our book with proceedings from the conference Nev and I arranged together with Eldred Jones in Freetown has been printed. I am posting a copy to you together with this letter. Another conference we had planned for this week had to be cancelled because of the military coup in Sierra Leone. I hope it does not detaroy our cooperation.

　　I got your new address from Suzanne Romaine, who has been a visiting professor at Uppsala this term.

　　　　With best wishes,

Karl Inge Sandred

Postadress - Postal address
Box 513
S - 751 20 UPPSALA

Besöksadress - Visiting address
Kyrkogårdsgatan 10

Telefon - Telephone
018 - 18 25 00 vx

some translations from Shakespeare and *The Bible*. I am a great admirer of his translation of Shakespeare's song from *Twelfth Night*, "O mistress mine, where are you roaming?". Decker realises the spirit of Shakespeare's lyric in very idiomatic and artistic Krio. His translation is not very widely known so I shall give both Shakespeare's song and Decker's translation of it:

> O mistress mine, where are you roaming?
> O, stay and hear; your true-love's coming,
>   That can sing both high and low:
> Trip no further, pretty sweeting;
> Journeys end in lovers meeting,
>   Every wise man's son doth know.
> What is love? 'Tis not hereafter;
> Present mirth hath present laughter;
>   What's to come is still unsure.
> In delay there lies no plenty;
> Then come kiss me, sweet and twenty,
>   Youth's a stuff will not endure.

Decker's version:

> Uspat yu de, mi yon yon pɔsin?
> Tinap, opin yu yes; yu rayt pɔsin
> De kam, we kin sing ɔl kaynaba sing.
> Mi fayn fayn lɔvin, yu waka dɔn dɔn.
> Wɛn tu rayt pɔsin mit, waka mɔs dɔn.
> Man we get sɛns no se dat na tru tin.
>
> Wetin na lɔv? Lɔv nɔto nɛks wɔl tin.
> Tide gladi gɛt tide yon laf.
> Nɔ put at pan tin we nɔ kam yet.
> Kam kis me ya, gud gud, ɛn plɛnti.
> Da tin we mek yu yɔng, i nɔba kip.

Some of Decker's translations are quite ingenious. Take the lines "What is love? 'Tis not hereafter;/ Present mirth hath present laughter;" Decker renders the half line " 'Tis not hereafter" as "nɔto nɛks wɔl tin". That word 'tin', like 'wan', will be found very useful by translators when they wish to express some abstract ideas. For instance, "the country's welfare" is often represented by "di kɔntri in bɛtɛ wan". Decker's treatment of the next line "Present mirth hath present laughter" is to my mind even more impressive. For 'present', he selects the word, "tide" and thus employs an extension of its meaning which is already present in the language. For instance, in the adage "Yu si tide yu nɔ si tumara" where "tide" and "tumara" represent the present and the future; and "gladi" for "mirth", the abstract concept of the source of laughter is also very good. "Tide gladi gɛt tide yon laf"—an excellent translation. Finally, in that poem, "Youth's a stuff will not endure;"—"youth", for which there is no single word in Krio, Decker translates with a periphrasis, "da ting we mek yu yɔng", thus ending with the line, "Da ting we mek yu yɔng, i nɔba kip". Decker has in fact transformed an abstract statement into a personal one, bringing in the word "yu". Of course, he could have used a word like "man" or "pɔsin" etc., but the direct address suits the spirit of this love lyric admirably.

Decker specifically states that his *Udat Di Kiap Fit* is an adaptation rather than a word-for-word translation. In spite of this he follows Shakespeare's text very closely and includes almost every speech. He abbreviates some and he omits one or two lines, but he does give himself the liberty of realising rather than translating and some of his realisations are interesting; he renders Shakespeare's line "What prodigal portion have I spent that I should come to such penury?" as "Wetin a du fɔ kam tɔn di prɔdigal sɔn?" That is not a translation; it assumes knowledge of the story of the prodigal son and merely makes reference to it. A more literal translation would have been something like this: "Us prɔdigal prɔpati a dɔn it fɔ mek naw a kam po so?"; "Us prɔdigal prɔpati we a it fɔ mek a kam po dis bad bad wan so?". Shakespeare has, "I pray thee Rosalind, sweet my coz, be merry"; Decker has, "Duya kɔzin Rozalin lus bɔdi". This to me is an excellent idiomatic Krio translation. Decker never translates the word 'banish'; he merely reproduces it in Krio as in this passage. The old Duke is banished by his younger brother, the new Duke. Decker has "Di nyu chif bin dɔn banish di ol chif we na in yon brɔda". He changes the passive voice to the active voice. *Corin*: "That is the way to make her scorn you still". Decker, attributing this speech to *Olman* has, "Na dat go mek i mek pan yu di mɔ" ('scorn' = 'mek pan'). A very good translation. A good example of Thomas Decker's adaptation is the song to Rosalind by Orlando in Act III Scene ii. The original version reads:

> From the east to western Ind,
> No jewel is like Rosalind.
> Her worth, being mounted on the wind,
> Through all the world bears Rosalind.

Krio has no word for the generalised term, 'jewel'. Indeed Krio is deficient in terms signifying types, categories etc. Decker solves the problem by substituting the more specific 'diamond' and he writes:

> Frɔm Kaylahun to Sulima
> Nɔn dayamɔn nɔ fayn lɛk Rozalin.
> Briz dɔn kɛr in fem ɔlɔbɔt;
> ɔlman na wɔl nɔ Rozalin.

Decker equally catches the spirit of the parody of such lines which the fool, Touchstone, called Yeliba in *Udat Di Kiap Fit*, makes a few lines later.

Shakespeare:

>If a hart do lack a hind,
>Let him seek out Rosalind.
>If the cat will after kind,
>So be sure will Rosalind.

Decker:

>If fritambo na bush wan wɛf,
>Mek i go luk fɔ Rozalin.
>If pus de luk fɔ in padi,
>Rozalin sɛf mɔs luk fɔ padi.

Decker's adaptation is set in Sierra Leone and consequently he ignores any possible charge of anachronism. So Shakespeare's 'pictures' becomes in Decker's translation 'fɔto'.

He handles the problems very well in this play and, in any case, any errors he may make in translation or in representing Shakespeare's original may not be vital in a light-hearted comedy. Translations become vital when they are of pieces of legislation or important government statements with sanctions and consequences attached. Some of these statements have technical terms for which there are no existing equivalents in Krio, and one must commend the newsreaders who, when confronted with complicated speeches and statements of this kind, have to do an on-the-spot translation from English texts. We have had some examples of this in the recent past. Newscasters had, for example, to translate 'The Economic Sabotage Act' and the very important statement of the Minister of Finance on the economy of the country into Sierra Leone languages, including Krio. I raised the question earlier about the intention of translating these statements into Sierra Leone languages. Presumably, it is to make these statements accessible to nationals, the great majority of whom would not understand English. We are concerned here specifically with Krio and it is presumed that somebody who does not understand English would find it very difficult to understand some of the long technical phrases which appear in the original if they were just reproduced in Krio. I must say that in spite of the incidence of clusters of English words it could still be argued that the newscaster is speaking Krio because this is the level of the language that is used between Krio speakers who have been educated in English, particularly when they are talking about subjects of a technical nature. They use the syntax and grammatical words of Krio but they spice their language with whole clusters of technical terms. This is what happens in a passage like the following, which bears all the marks of a running translation. The newscaster comes across the phrase, ''a surplus of revenue over expenditure'', and he translates this as ''sɔplɔs ɔf rɛvɛnyu oba wetin wi go gɛt fɔ spend''. He fails to translate 'revenue' but makes up for it by translating 'expenditure'.

He is obviously quite capable of translating but he is handicapped because he is working under pressure; if he had had time to actually translate it and read from a translation he would no doubt have found the equivalent for 'revenue'. He might have had to recast the whole passage into something like, 'Wi no go ekspɛkt fɔ gɛt mɔni lɛf na wi an afta wi dɔn spɛnd ɔl wetin wi go gɛt fɔ spɛnd'. This kind of periphrasis may be necessary if the translation has to make sense to people who have no education in English, and presumably at whom such a translation is targeted. A similar borrowing of whole phrases from the English text into the Krio translation can be seen in the following: "The President warned you about the need to *change direction for the better* and adopt *strong* positive *economic reform measures* and instil a *strong sense of national discipline* in the management of the country's finances." "Di Prɛsident bin wɔn wi se wi fɔ *chenj dirɛkshɔn fɔ di bɛtɛ;* wi fɔ gɛt *strɔng ikɔnɔmik rifɔm mɛzhɔ* en gɛt *strɔng sɛns* ɔf *nashɔnal disiplin* na di kɔntri in kɔpɔ biznɛs."

One also comes across passages in a translation where the translator actually changes his mind and produces a second word which he considers more appropriate than the first. In an otherwise good rendering, he wishes to translate the Minister's "we are prepared. . . to expel as many non-citizens"; he says, "Gɔvament go ɛkspɛl, drɛb kɔmɔt na dis kɔntri dɛm wan dɛm we nɔ bɔn ya so"; obviously, he realises that "ɛkspɛl" may not be readily intelligible to some of his listeners and he changes his mind in mid-stream. If he had had time he would have balanced the alternatives and decided on either 'ɛkspɛl' or 'drɛb kɔmɔt' but not on both. The two passages read:

We are prepared to shut down as many shops as possible and to expel as many non-citizens who do not want to cooperate. . .

Wi go rɛdi fɔ lɔk bɔku bɔku shap en ɛkspɛl drɛb kɔmɔt na dis kɔntri dɛm wan dɛm we nɔ bɔn na ya so we nɔ wan fɔ jɔynan wit Gɔvament. . .

Some of the best efforts of the translator are represented by a passage like the following:

Now I want to talk to the exploiters of this economy, citizens and non-citizens. . .

Naw a wan fɔ tɔk to dɛm wan we tek dis kɔntri mek famyad, ɛn du wetin dɛm wan fɔ du; sɔm na ya dɛm bɔn, sɔm ɔf dɛm nɔ bɔn na ya. . .

Here he breaks completely loose from the shackles of the original English and becomes accessible to every level of Krio speaker. These passages are cited not in adverse criticism of the translator but to highlight some of the difficulties with which he has to contend. In the circumstances, this particular translation is most commendable. I also listened to the Krio translation of the recent Currency Control and Economic Sabotage Act, and have the same impression of a very creditable job which could have been even better done.

The problems of the translator lead me to suggest two things: First, that translators of such important statements or pieces of legislation should be given their copy in good time so that they can do a proper translation before going on the air. Secondly, even if they had time, they would encounter problems and these problems arise simply because Krio is being stretched to cover areas it had not covered in its previous existence. Therefore, it is necessary for an on-going workshop of experts to look at various areas of vocabulary and see to what extent they can offer intelligible Krio equivalents for them. If Krio is to bear the freight that it is being called upon to bear, then this is an urgent necessity.

Other papers deal with questions of orthography and the problems of reading from a Krio script and with the problem of a standardised orthography. Some attempts have been made to standardise the orthography, the results of which are to be found in the *Krio-English Dictionary*[4], which should be a useful guide to users of the language. It is unfortunately, in its present form, a very expensive volume and I do not expect many people to possess individual copies, but because of this and because of the importance that Krio is assuming, copies of this *Dictionary* must be available to those who write and read the language. Thus public libraries and certain institutions should have copies even if they have to be chained to the desks to prevent them from being taken away. Several active users of Krio have never even seen the *Dictionary*; this is not surprising because the original published price of twenty pounds sterling put it out of the reach of the great majority of potential users, but the current price of fifty pounds sterling puts it almost beyond the reach of every likely user in the country except institutions. I must therefore urge institutions to invest in copies for the use of their staff and the public. I say this quite unshamedly because Professor Fyle and I get no royalties whatever from sales.

---

[4] Fyle, C.N. and Jones, E.D., 1980, *A Krio English Dictionary*, Oxford and Freetown: Oxford University Press and Sierra Leone University Press.

JULIUS S. SPENCER

Factors Militating against the Easy Reading and Writing of Krio in the Theatre

Introduction

In 1957, Eldred Jones made a call for the development of literature in Krio because he was convinced that a large number of people in Sierra Leone

... are completely cut off from at least one source of aesthetic experience, because they are not sufficiently in command of the language which they are compelled by circumstances to speak.[1]

In making this call, Professor Jones was merely echoing what people like the late Thomas Decker had been advocating for years. Decker's commitment to the fight for recognition of Krio as ". . . a living language flexible enough for artistic expression"[2] and as a language worthy of respect, earned him the appellation "crusader for Krio" by a correspondent writing for *West Africa* in 1965.[3] Thomas Decker's fight spanned a period of about three decades and took the form of numerous newspaper articles, particularly in the *Daily Guardian* of which he eventually became editor, and the writing of poems and plays in Krio. While there were other people like Gladys Casely-Hayford, who used Krio in creative writing, Thomas Decker's work can easily be regarded as the most influential.

In 1964, Decker translated Shakespeare's *Julius Caesar* into Krio, and the play was performed in the grounds of State House by the National Theatre League, an umbrella organisation for theatrical activities in the country at that time. In translating *Julius Caesar* into Krio, Decker's aim was twofold:

First to make propaganda for the Krio language by proving that the most serious things can be written and spoken in it, and secondly, to make it possible for people who did not have the opportunity of reading Shakespeare at school to taste of the excellence of this great writer by seeing one of his most popular plays staged in their own language.[4]

---

[1] E.D. Jones, "The Potentialities of Krio as a Literary Language", *Sierra Leone Studies*, No. 9, pp. 40—48, Dec. 1957.

[2] L. Spitzer, *The Creoles of Sierra Leone*, University of Wisconsin Press, 1974, pp. 144—145.

[3] "Crusader for Krio", *West Africa*, Aug. 14, 1965, p. 903.

[4] T. Decker, in an introductory note for a privately mimeographed edition of *Udat Di Kiap Fit* (no date provided).

Due to the fact that the use of State House as the venue gave the performance an elitist status, it is doubtful whether Thomas Decker achieved his second objective. His first objective, however, was most certainly achieved, for this production marked the birth of theatre in Krio. Decker later wrote a Krio adaptation of another Shakespeare play, this time *As You Like It*, which he called *Udat Di Kiap Fit*. These efforts proved that Krio could be a vehicle for the expression of serious thought and could be used in literary endeavours.

The case for the use of Krio in the theatre received a further boost in 1968 when Juliana John (now Mrs Rowe), a member of the cast for the production of *Julius Ceasar* in Krio, wrote and directed *Na Mami Bohn Am* and in 1969 *I Dey I Noh Du*. These plays took drama in Krio a step further in that they, unlike Thomas Decker's plays, were not translations or adaptations, but original full-length plays dealing with current social issues and fully embedded in Krio culture. These two plays became immensely popular with Freetown audiences, thus vindicating Thomas Decker and others like him in the long fight for the recognition of Krio as a language capable of expressing serious thought. The work of Thomas Decker and Juliana John thus served as eye-openers for budding playwrights and theatre artists, and is largely responsible for the deluge of Krio plays that has since characterized the theatre in Sierra Leone.

The Orthography and the Theatre in Krio

More than any other genre of creative writing in Sierra Leone, drama can claim pre-eminence in the area of Krio literature. By sheer volume alone, it can easily be regarded as the most popular medium for writing in the language. It is therefore perhaps not surprising that the problems faced by the theatre in Krio are numerous. One of the most persistent problems has been that of the orthography. Since the birth of Krio drama, playwrights and actors have been facing problems in writing and reading scripts. For a long time, these problems stemmed from the absence of a standardized orthography for the language. All the efforts so far at achieving a standardization of the orthography, however, do not seem to have solved the problem.

The absence of an orthography for Krio in its early years stemmed from the fact that it was for a long time only a spoken language, and so the need for an orthography was not felt. When, however, people began writing in Krio, they drew on their knowledge of English to create what Neville Shrimpton calls "mixed orthographies".[5] These orthographies, which still exist, rely

---

[5] N. Shrimpton, "Au (Aw?) fo (foh?) rayt (rait? write?) Krio?", *West Africa*, March 1, 1982, pp. 561—563.

heavily on English spelling conventions, and display numerous inconsistencies which make it difficult for an individual to master them. Unfortunately, it is still these mixed orthographies that are most widely used.

The first attempt at creating an orthography which displayed a consistency of symbols, was made by Thomas Decker. He created a semi-phonemic orthography for his *Udat Di Kiap Fit*,[6] and this orthography was picked up by a few other theatre practitioners. Unfortunately, apart from theatre groups such as "Lekomide dem", whose director was Juliana John, and Tabule Theatre, the vast majority of groups in existence in the 1970s were unaware of the existence of this orthography. It was therefore never widely used, In groups where it was used, it greatly facilitated the writing and reading of Krio.

The publication by C.N. Fyle and E.D. Jones of their *Krio-English Dictionary* (1980) marked the beginning of another stage in the search for a standardized Krio orthography, and except for a few modifications, the orthography used in this dictionary has been recommended as the standard Krio orthography. One would expect that, with the coming into being of such an orthography, the problems facing theatre practitioners working in Krio would be greatly reduced. Unfortunately, however, the problems continue to exist undiminished. We shall, therefore, now examine these problems.

Problems

It seems to me that one of the major causes of the problems facing playwrights and actors is the lack of knowledge about the recommended standard orthography for Krio. It is a shame that five years after the recommendations were made, not many people outside academia are conversant with the details of even the alphabet. No efforts seem to have been made to inform or educate theatre practitioners, who it is acknowledged are the greatest users of the written form of Krio, about the workings of the Krio orthography. Little wonder then that while 87.5 % of the respondents to a questionnaire on the use of Krio in the theatre were aware of the existence of a standardized orthography for Krio, only 58.3 % actually made use of it. In addition, only 50 % of those who made use of the orthography, consistently used all the letters. The recommended standard orthography has obviously not caught on well. Despite the fact that some theatre groups and individuals have mastered it and use it consistently, for the majority of practitioners this is not the case. In fact, even those who use the orthography consistently still encounter problems.

From personal experience, and the experience of several other theatre prac-

---

[6] This translation is forthcoming as Volume 7 in the *Krio Publications Series*.

titioners who currently use the recommended standard Krio orthography, the source of all the problems encountered in writing or reading the language is the symbols used to represent vowel and diphthong sounds. In the first place, from the writer's perspective, the presence of the phonetic symbols ɔ, ɛ, and ŋ poses two problems. The first one is a practical one which makes it difficult for writers to disseminate their work. Typing scripts which make use of these symbols either has to be done using a special typewriter, which most playwrights do not have access to, or the phonetic symbols have to be hand-written: a tedious and at times frustrating experience. The second problem is lack of familiarity with these phonetic symbols, which causes writers to be daunted by the effort required to master their use. One should not overlook the fact that for the vast majority of playwrights there would have been no encounter with these or any other phonetic symbols prior to encountering the Krio orthography.

These two problems thus combine to produce, in some cases, a complete disregard for the phonetic symbols, and the use of other more familiar symbols such as *e* for *ɛ* and *o* for *ɔ*; *ŋ* of course is completely ignored, and all words containing this sound are spelt with an *n*. This certainly is not a satisfactory state of affairs, for when this happens, the orthography ceases to be phonemic, and for non-native speakers, learning to read and write the language becomes more difficult.

Neville Shrimpton says, in his introduction to *Queen Esther* by Esther Taylor-Pearce,[7]

. . . since English is the official language of government and education in Sierra Leone, just about anyone who needs to write anything down in Krio will be conversant with English.

This issue is central to an understanding of the problems being encountered by theatre practitioners in the reading and writing of Krio, as will presently be shown.

Theatre practitioners in Sierra Leone have, almost without exception, had some formal education. As a result, they are all at least basically literate in English. Instinctively, therefore, there is the general tendency to spell and pronounce English words as in English. Thus, apart from the difficulties encountered with the phonetic symbols in reading Krio, there is the added difficulty of having to pronounce the same combination of letters in different ways. In this regard, the greatest offender is the diphthong *ai*.

From an observation of actors reading scripts in Krio, it is obvious to me that a large proportion of them persistently encounter problems with words containing the *ai* diphthong. Even among those fairly conversant with the or-

---

[7] *Krio Publications Series*, Vol. 3, p. vi.

thography, occasional stumblings over such words do occur. The problem seems to be most marked with words ending in this diphthong. As noted earlier, this problem stems from the fact that all theatre practitioners have a background of education in English. They are therefore familiar with words such as *may, say, day, bay* etc. When words with the same spelling are encountered in Krio, the instinctive reaction is to pronounce them with the *e* vowel rather than the *ai* diphthong. This, as would be expected, creates confusion and persistently disrupts the flow of the reading, making it difficult for both the reader and listener to decipher the meaning of sentences in which such words occur.

The problems encountered by playwrights and actors using Krio can therefore be seen to stem from two main factors: lack of familiarity with the standard orthography and the symbols used to represent vowel and diphthong sounds. Both these factors combine to make the writing and reading of Krio a difficult and at times frustrating experience for large numbers of theatre practitioners. This need not be so, and cannot continue if the reading and writing of Krio should become widespread. In fact, if a real standardization of the orthography is to be achieved, not only among theatre practitioners, but among the general populace, then it is my firm belief that some modifications need to be made to the recommended orthography.

Suggestions

The saying "practice makes perfect" is a truism, the validity of which in the area of language use cannot be questioned. However, at times, the amount of practice required for the attainment of proficiency can prove to be a hindrance rather than a help, for frustration could set in and cause a cessation of effort, especially if the individual's level of motivation is not particularly high, and there are no sanctions for failure. This needs to be borne in mind whilst attempts are being made to popularize the use of a standardized Krio orthography. In the first place, more effective methods need to be adopted to create an awareness of the existence of a recommended standard orthography, and to ensure that potential users fully understand the workings of this orthography. So far, the only effort in this direction has been that manifested in the *Krio Publications Series*. There needs to be a lot more of this. In other words, we need a lot more Krio publications, and local ones too. While the work being done by Umeå University needs to be highly commended, it must be pointed out that for the vast majority of the actual users of the written form of the language, the *Krio Publications Series* is totally inaccessible, and therefore not very useful. What is needed is local production of material which would be widely disseminated so potential users become aware of the recommended orthography and become used to reading Krio.

As earlier stated, the greatest percentage of writing and reading of Krio currently takes place in the theatre. There is thus a growing body of Krio literature which is inaccessible to the general populace in written form. In order to facilitate the growth of this literature and make the reading and writing of Krio easier for actors and playwrights, and subsequently the potentially large reading audience, some elements of the recommended orthography need to be changed.

The above discussion has shown that the use of the phonetic symbols ɔ, ε and ŋ and the *ai* diphthong, which currently is written as *ay*, pose problems for playwrights and actors. I therefore suggest that these four symbols be changed.

Fyle and Jones suggest in their *Krio-English Dictionary* that "a practical device for ordinary purposes is to write both *e* and *ε* as *e*, and both *o* and *ɔ* as *o*".[8] However, when one considers the possibility of encountering sentences such as

Bo, da wan de no get det. Na bet dem bet am. In fakt sef, dem bot am.

the assertion that the context will disambiguate the very few instances where confusion may occur, becomes questionable. I suggest that the method employed by Decker in his orthography be adopted. Decker uses *ey* to represent the *e* sound, and *e* to represent the *ε* sound. The *ɔ* sound he represents by *oh*. This would solve the practical problem of typing and also get rid of the phonetic symbols which tend to scare away potential users; ŋ should also be expunged from the orthography, and the sound represented by *ng*.[9]

With regard to the problematic *ai* diphthong, I would suggest that it be represented by *ai* rather than *ay*, particularly when it occurs at the end of a word. Thus, we will have *bai, dai, sai*, etc. It is perhaps worth mentioning that a large number of theatre practitioners prefer this. There are some instances, however, where *ay* may be more appropriate. These would be cases where the *y* sound is more pronounced than the *i* sound. Words like *ayen* or *faya* for example could justifiably be spelt like this.

In conclusion, I would like to state that I am not a linguist or a phonologist, and I am not trying to pose as one either. I am a theatre practitioner. It is my belief, however, that the onus of deciding on an orthography for Krio should not lie solely with linguists or phonologists, for I do not believe that it is only

---

[8] C.N. Fyle and E.D. Jones, *A Krio-English Dictionary*, Oxford and Freetown: Oxford University Press and Sierra Leone University Press, 1980, p. xx.

[9] These suggestions came up in the subsequent discussions and the consensus was that the phonetic characters ε and ɔ be retained and ŋ discarded [editors' note].

linguistic or phonological considerations that should come into play. I have therefore tried to highlight what to me are factors affecting, in a negative way, our use of the written form of Krio.

RAYMOND E. DE-SOUZA GEORGE

Problems Relating to Reading from a Script
(with Special Reference to Broadcasters, Actors and Other Readers)

The Krio people and Krio, the language they speak, have been the focus of much discussion since the abolition of slavery. Circumstances of history, communication and necessary socialization, including commerce in particular, have taken us beyond such questions as: "Is Krio a language?"—thus the tongue of the Liberated Africans now serves Sierra Leone as the *lingua franca.*

In spite of the foregoing, the problems surrounding the establishment of Krio as a complete medium of communication have still not yet been fully solved. They haunt every stratum of our society, particularly the academic/ literate community in its dealings with written material, which has to be assimilated through decodable symbols which form the primary tools for reading. However, the facility of reading is not a monopoly of people who only have a professional interest in the language. Native and non-native users in various walks of life may at some time or other have reason to read a script in Krio.

The written form of any language must have as its starting-point a system of symbols, its orthography, which determines its ability to serve as a communication channel. Impinging on this system are problems relating to writing, printing, publication and reading. In Sierra Leone, users have been combating the systems of inherited symbols while trying to introduce indigenous phonetic symbols against the background of the considerable influence exerted by our inherited European languages. Specifically for Krio, these problems are made all the more enormous because of ingrained attitudes to the language, which are primarily a result of historical stigma and prejudices built up as a consequence of the social affiliation of the Creoles during the colonial era, particularly in the realms of administration and politics.

In a modest way I intend to indicate some of these problems which I have been able to highlight through interviews and discussions which constitute the only source of data for this paper. I hope to say how they affect the reading of a Krio script by people in the different walks of life mentioned above. Attitudes of users play a great part in the development of a language, and this aspect has also occupied my attention. Recommendations on the question of establishing a standardized orthography have definitely preceded this workshop, but it would still be in place to advance suggestions for those recommendations to be more dynamically utilized. My attempt to attend to these issues will, as earlier indicated, avoid references to any previous document.

Broadcasters are in the business of communication perhaps merely as one-way instruments whose use and concern or involvement with the language may not be in the same vein as that of the creative artist. Unhappily, some of these broadcasters have never read a script in Krio, the most popularly employed medium in or out of official discourse, and mostly translate live from an English script. Relying as they do entirely on sound without visual support, they need to learn the orthography of whatever language they use. Since radio is the medium through which the majority of the population is reached, it is most important that the material is accurately transmitted.

The Sierra Leone Broadcasting Service (SLBS) under its present Director General may have seen the need for the kind of education hinted at above. It has therefore set up a Broadcasting Advisory Committee which embraces the Language and Religious Advisory Committees. The first of the two sub-committees is charged with the responsibility of examining the issue of orthographies for the various indigenous languages in order to make recommendations and to advise on a standard for the Sierra Leone Broadcasting Service.

This is a step in the right direction as my discussions also led me to the discovery that most broadcasters prefer reading from scripts written in English, a mental block which militates against the desire and the ability to read in Krio. The absence as yet, of either an accepted standard orthography or uniformly adopted mode of delivery, points to yet another embargo in the way of generating and developing interest in the formal aspects of the language.

The aim of broadcasters in past years seems to have been to mimic the delivery of English native speakers. In my view, this must have helped to establish a false sense of what is right or proper, and could also have built up a sub-conscious resistance to the use of indigenous languages on formal occasions. Now all this has changed and indigenous languages are more generally accepted. This augurs well for Krio as a broadcasting medium, as I am sure the Language Advisory Committee will push for the adoption of an orthography and training in reading. Some of the programmes in Krio are, however, plagued by problems of translation and interpretation, as *The News, We Den Se, Fo Wil Ɛn Tu Fut* and the like illustrate. A popular panelist habitually uses *patikla* to mean 'particularly', instead of translating it as 'nɔ lɛk we'. This, however, is not his only lapse, but unfortunately many regard him as an authority. Another broadcaster, who I am sure must have been reading in Krio from an English script, lifted 'to delegate' from the English into his Krio translation. One refreshing aspect of our discussions, however, is the fact that broadcasters are themselves aware of these limitations and welcome as a necessary and urgent measure the drive to standardize broadcasting in general.

Like broadcasters, actors must pay particular attention to their delivery. Being creative communicators, to whom the spoken word and written word are as important as their bodies in giving meaning and life to what they see on the page, they must, like broadcasters, be concerned with the effective use of language. As such, a script becomes the actor's invaluable tool.

In my experience in Sierra Leone, many actors tend to neglect the script once they have formed a slight acquaintance with it. Because of this attitude to the script, they do not feel the need to become conversant with the orthography of the language in which they are performing. It is now necessary for actors to master the orthography of Krio, which is the dominant language in the Sierra Leone theatre today.

An actor of many years' standing, who has also written and directed a play, said to me that the issue of an orthography should be left to the choice of the user since he did not really see it as a problem. It was therefore not a matter of urgency. However, when I pointed out to him that the orthography of any language is the backbone of its written form and a guarantee of its orderly development and continuity, he agreed that there is a need for users to learn the standard orthography. For this actor the principle of convenience could solve the issue of an orthography, that is, each actor would use English symbols and develop his own idiosyncratic spelling of Krio. This would clearly lead to confusion and create more problems in the reading of the language.

I myself started with this principle of convenience but quickly discovered the value of using the standard orthography. Perhaps this is a path which other actors will have to follow. Many of the Krio playwrights are completely unaware of the existence of a Krio orthography, and since they are often responsible within their theatre groups for directing as well as training the actors, they merely perpetuate their ignorance. If actors are not just interested in acting but also see the need to use their creative talent in writing, then there is a further need for them to acquire a facility in the use of the standard orthography. As with every skill, such a facility will grow with practice. The following statement reproduced in three different orthographies below is meant to illustrate the progress from an idiosyncratic convenience orthography to the standard orthography, a path which I followed:

(1) Borbor, nar we yone done kam so tiday (teeday).
(2) Bohboh, na wi yon dohn kam so tidey.
(3) Bɔbɔ, na wi yon dɔn kam so tide.
    (My boy, our own people have come here today.)

However, most readers, no matter what their backgrounds are, seem to have doubts about the use of certain letters or combinations of letters recommended for the standard orthography. There is a problem of confusion arising in some cases because of the influence of English spelling, for example:

The difficulty caused by the use of the digraph *ay*, which is pronounced as /ei/ in English *day*, but as /ai/ in the Krio word with the same spelling (*day* meaning 'die').

The use of *e* for the close /e/ sound in Krio, leading to confusion with regard to the pronunciation of Krio words like *wet*, pronounced /wet/, which translates English 'wait' and *not* 'wet'.

The problem of recognizing and using the reversed *c* (ɔ), as in *bɔbɔ* (English 'boy') in the sentence above. This is a sound which is close to that of the vowel in English *bought*.

These are just a few of the symbols which create problems for readers, especially new readers. The above symbols are used in the following example, again illustrating the gradual development from the convenient, through Decker, to the Jones and Fyle orthography—the standard.

(1) Waitin make you lef di dog for die nar trit (treet)?
(2) Weytin meyk yu lef di dohg foh dai na trit?
(3) Wetin mek yu lɛf di dɔg fɔ day na trit?
   (Why did you leave the dog to die in the street?)

For this paper the third category of users embraces individuals from a wide cross-section of disciplines and walks of life. Some have a professional commitment to the language while others can generally be seen as casual users. Among this category of users I hardly found any evidence of more than a passive interest in the language.

There are certain attitudes which have long prevailed among Sierra Leoneans in general. Any form of speech in school which gives the slightest note of interference with one's ability to grasp and use the English language was banned. This ban on the spoken word must have done irreparable harm to the use of Krio and other indigenous languages because it reduced them to a second-class status. I do not know how effective the pilot programme for the use of Krio in primary schools has been but the prejudice against the language still continues in schools. When we discourage our children from expressing themselves in their mother tongue, we are aiding in their deculturalization and are also impeding their linguistic development.

Even among native speakers, Krio is a kind of leper in decent communication and has to be kept out of sight and hearing. This means that any sense of pride that either the language or its culture might invest in an individual or group is effectively undermined. The result is that most of the efforts that have been made to standardize the language and give it respectability have been largely ineffective. This is regrettable because a people who cannot read or do not want to read will not see the need for preserving written historical records. If we are to reverse this trend we must develop the language for effective dissemination.

In our midst today there are a number of non-governmental agencies which use theatre for the purpose of message dissemination. Generally they use Krio. Their argument for being guided by the principle of convenience is that the bulk of their target group is either not literate or barely literate and hardly aware of a Krio orthography. They would therefore not be wise to sacrifice the aim and objective of their projects simply to do linguistic favours for Krio. I believe that the justification of their argument is brought out in the following example from a UNICEF poster: "Udat born me wae nor marklate me?" (Who was it that brought me into the world but did not have me inoculated?) The question implies the importance of timely inoculation. "Marklate" the most important word in the question is a combination of "mark" and "late"—two elements which are separately misleading but when fused together and pronounced become intelligible. The use of the standard orthography would give the following result: "Udat bɔn mi we nɔ maklet mi?"

This would present problems for almost everybody except those fully acquainted with this orthography. Even the use of the Decker orthography would not adequately satisfy both agency and target group: "Udat bohn mi wey noh makleyt mi?" Only when the standard orthography has been universally adopted would the need for expedient alternatives be eliminated.

Finally, the primary problem is not the failure to understand the technicality of formalizing the language, but the prevailing attitudes to the oral language itself. This has induced a tendency to automatically reject the language as being unsuitable for anything other than colloquial use. The situation has not been truly positively helped because opinions are still not all complimentary to the endeavour to use Krio as a language of instruction in our educational system. In other words, fundamental to these negative attitudes is a deeply induced sense of inferiority.

In the light of the foregoing, I would like to advance the following recommendations:

a) that a campaign be launched for the oral and written use of our indigenous languages through the dissemination of the standard orthography.

b) that the SLBS should reintroduce educational programmes such as Mende and/or Temne by radio, both on radio and television for all the indigenous languages.

c) that workshops for various classes of professional and amateur communicators be run with a view to reinforcing their commitment to what I see not only as a linguistic struggle but a cultural reawakening.

ERIC JOHNSON
Problems Relating to the Publication of Krio Materials

According to Dr. David Dalby's report, *Draft Recommendation to the Sierra Leone Ministry of Education on the Use of National Languages in Education* (David Dalby, 26th October, 1980), Krio is an African Language (page 2 specific proposals, paragraph I). Also, in the *Journal of Education*, published by the Ministry of Education, Vol. 10 No. 2 of October 1975, on p. 9, paragraph (b), the contributor, Professor Clifford Fyle, under the title "A National Language Policy and the Teacher of English in Sierra Leone", observes that "Krio is the common *lingua franca* in this country". Krio is used as an intertribal vehicle of verbal communication in trade, politics, education, domestic and other social activities (*Journal of Education*, Vol. 10, No. 2 of 1975, pp. 7—9). This use is spread throughout the country reaching the nothernmost town of Kabala, the easternmost district of Kono, the western districts of Port Loko and Kambia, as well as Bo in the centre of the country. Apart from the predominantly Krio-speaking western area, there is hardly any district headquarter town in the country where some amount of Krio is not spoken.

Unfortunately, the Krio language, the use of which has increased steadily over the last two hundred years, is still very limited in printed form for mainly technical reasons which are discussed below.

Printing presses in Sierra Leone are not equipped with phonetic symbols and therefore printers cannot accept jobs written in the Krio orthography. Even the Bunumbu Press in Bo, which pioneered the printing and publishing of books and pamphlets in Sierra Leonean languages such as Mende and Temne, has been unable to undertake such printing for some time now. The NEWCO photo-copying and printing company in Freetown, which had produced *Mi Fɔs Ridin Buk* (*My First Reading Book Series*) Books I and II, published by the Indigenous Languages Unit of the Ministry of Education in conjunction with UNESCO in 1984, could not undertake a reprint two years later. The reason was the inability to obtain special printing "plates", the same problem encountered by Bunumbu Press. For financial reasons, very few typewriters in the country are fitted with phonetic characters. One or two (the number is unknown) may be found in the two constituent colleges of the University and Milton Margai Teachers' College. Our Indigenous Languages Unit at the Ministry had two such typewriters, one in the Freetown office and another in the Mende Zone at Bo. There is none as yet in the Temne Zone Office at Port Loko and none in the Limba Zone Office at Makeni. Therefore, the two phonetic typing machines were serving the four language zones in the country, though inadequately. The situation was made even worse when a fire in our Bo office destroyed the Mende Zone machine. The Ministry's Indigenous Languages Unit very badly needs a couple of such machines if the language work is not to suffer further vitiation.

Many intending Krio writers would need training in the orthography, spelling patterns and idioms of the language. Some of these matters are dealt with, for example, in Professor Alex Johnson's paper "Varieties of Krio and Standard Krio" and Mr Ajayi Coomber's "The New Krio Orthography and Some Unresolved Problems" in this volume. Editors, typists and printers should also be given some training in the use of written Krio. Such training would enhance local publishing and printing, thus bringing down costs, saving on foreign exchange and cutting down the time lag between composition and distribution to readers.

Many potential Krio writers might prefer to write in an international language, English or French, rather than their mother tongue, Krio, even though their material may be purely Krio-orientated. They may feel that an international language brings greater prestige and financial rewards. But Krio, in contrast to other Sierra Leonean languages, not only has a wide potential readership within Sierra Leone but may also have some currency outside the country's borders in Liberia, Nigeria, The Gambia and Guinea. In any case, works written in local languages could be translated into international languages and thus secure for their authors an even greater readership and renown. There are only a few Krio writers to set a standard for future writers, but the plays, poems and short stories of writers like Dele Charley, Donald Mackay, Kashor Woode and Chris During, should point the way. There are also quite a number of budding writers whose works are as yet unknown or unpublished.

There is a great need for textbooks in Krio from primary to college level. The problem here is that the subject experts may have no linguistic training and may thus not be able to transfer concepts in their subject areas into Krio. Here there may be a need for extensive borrowing of vocabulary items into Krio. So great is the need for learners to acquire basic concepts in their mother tongue that an extensive training programme is necessary for subject experts to be able to transfer such concepts—mathematical, geographical, legal, scientific etc.—into Krio. If newspapers are to be printed in Krio and have substantial columns of Krio incorporated into them, the presses must be fitted with phonetic characters. Editors, reporters and even news-vendors should all be trained in the use of standardized Krio and its idioms. Because the readers of such publications would not be familiar with the new orthography, books and newspapers should contain a short guide to pronunciation such as is given on the first inside page of *Gud Yus Fɔ ɔlman.*

Although there is quite a fund of folk material in Krio, very little of this appears in print and many of today's children do not even know of it. A few examples of such stories are "Lɛf am de, na de yu mit am", a story about a man and a ghost lady, "Wan fut jombi", a tale about a one-legged fairy character, and "Yɔŋkɔn pas mi dɔla lɔs", the adventures of a crafty notorious rogue. Some of these were of a local or zonal character. For example, there was a story told about a mountain village farmer, whose wife gave birth to half a dozen crippled children as God's punishment for his cruelty to animals (goats and sheep), whose legs he used to break and maim whenever they poached on his vegetables. The devils of Fore Wata of York seaside village and Orogu Bridge at Hastings village all had their own stories framed about them. Even, a not-so-old story is told about the colonial rediffusion radio box receiver which, on coming on and saying loudly "Good afternoon everybody", caused a thief inside the house to apologize to it in Krio saying, "A beg sa" meaning "I am sorry, sir". He thought it was the owner of the house that had arrived home from work.

It is disappointing that very few stories of people's experiences of places and things are written down. Many of our Krio children are in consequence not trained to imagine and create their own stories. The stories they know and can tell are mostly exotic ones from European and other African countries, or from other tribal areas in this country, which have been read or told to them.

It would not be amiss, as part of the literary aspect of Krio publishing to give some training also in the framing of stories, poems, comics and songs from common as well as strange incidents; religious, legal, medical, commercial, social episodes, displays of wit or stupidity as in *Dandogo*.

Similarly, very few Krio songs are written and published although people enjoy and appreciate them in performance. The following are examples of old Krio songs.

TITI BORE
Titi Bore go Watalo
Fɔ go bay fange.
Wɛn Titi Bore go,
I mit fange pɔt dɔn dɔn.
Wɛn Titi Bore lɛf Watalo
I fɔdɔm na Estin Rod.
Aliluya, wat a Sevyɔ.

DA TREN FƆ BO

Da tren fɔ Bo
I nɔ wan gri fɔ go.
Da tren fɔ Bo
I nɔ wan gri fɔ go.
Da tren fɔ Bo i taya
Bikɔs i nɔ gɛt faya;
Da tren fɔ Bo
I nɔ wan gri fɔ go.

AKPA UMAN DUYA

Akpa uman duya,
Put yu akpa dɔng.
Akpa uman duya,
Put yu akpa dɔng.
Bay yu wan sɛnt jinja;
Bay yu wan kɔp shuga;
Mek yu jinjabia swit.
Yɛnki bɔy go bay am.

US SUP SERA KUKU TIDE?

Us sup Sera kuk tide?
Na sawa sawa.
Us sup Sera kuk tide?
Na sawa sawa.
Us sup Sera kuk tide?
Na sawa sawa, nɛvamayn krenkre.
Us sup i kuk tide?
Na sawa sawa, nɛvamayn krenkre.

Seemingly the Krios do not appear to be prolific in secular song creation unlike other tribes in Sierra Leone who have songs connected with farming, fishing and weaving activities. Even during rice pounding (polishing) there are Mende and Temne songs accompanying the dropping of the pestle into the mortar. This is not so with Krio. Perhaps an exception to this is the washerwoman's song during the 'cornstick' brushing operation:

Pe mi fɔ dis,
Nɔ gi mi mɔ.
Shu shu shu shu.
Pe mi fɔ dis,
Nɔ gi mi egen.
Shu shu shu shu.

Even so-called Krio religious songs are rarely in Krio throughout. Most so-called Krio shouts or choruses are either in English or a mixture of Krio and English. This Krio funeral shout is an example:

> Aw yu manej to climb Jekɔb lɛda?
> Aw yu manej to climb Jekɔb lɛda?
> Aw yu manej to climb Jekɔb lɛda?
> Aw yu manej we yu rich om?

At wedding entertainments a song about the bride would go like this:

> Udat yu gi am to?
> A gi am to da lili bɔy tonayt.

These problems could be overcome through: (a) training in the use of the orthography, (b) the use of Krio sentence structures and idioms, (c) seeing song possibilities in common happenings, (d) the help of qualified musicians, particularly those specialized in African music, since not all Krio words sing well with certain musical notes.

There is a biblical saying, "A prophet is not without honour save in his own country." Perhaps that may serve as a reminder for us to recall the hawker's warning from the late Mr Currey, famous coffee and cocoa seller of the 1930s and 40s: "Patronize your own, realize your own." Many of us Sierra Leoneans tend to show an avid preference for things foreign while looking down on our own.

This could be a problem in getting people to appreciate publications in Krio, and to pay a realistic, rational price for a textbook, novel or even a newspaper. If these prejudices are to be overcome, readers have to be induced to buy Krio material. Such publications may have to be initially subsidized to make them cheaply available, as was done in the case of the *Gud Yus Fɔ ɔlman* (The New Testament), which, as a result, has become very popular not only in the Western Area but also in some provincial Mende and Temne churches.

A few Krio workshops have been conducted for primary school teachers and Freetown Teachers' Training College lecturers. The workshops were mounted in turn by the Indigenous Languages Unit of the Ministry of Education, in collaboration with UNESCO and by URBS (University Research Bureau Services) in collaboration with the Indigenous Languages Unit and the Institute of Education. Out of half a dozen workshops only one was for textbook-writing and another for the writing of supplementary materials. The only works printed from these activities are the *Mi Fɔs Ridin Buk* series, Books I and II, now in use in pilot Krio teaching schools. This is grossly inadequate. Following on the successful evaluation of the Krio, Mende, Temne and Limba languages teaching in 1989, the teaching should now naturally proceed from pilot stage to full national dissemination. This makes it imperative for many more texts series to be written to cover the whole of primary one to six and the whole secondary range on to university. Again the need for training, research and the collecting of materials must be emphasized.

Krio, Mende, Limba and Temne are being taught on a pilot basis in some

40 schools spread all over the country at present. Religious bodies such as the Institute of Sierra Leonean Languages and the United Christian Council are engaged in some writing in one or other of the Sierra Leonean languages. The Sierra Leone Association of University women has an interest in textbook writing in Krio. Also, many drama groups are busy writing and acting plays in Krio. It is, however, lamentable that there are no established houses for the publication of writings in Sierra Leonean languages. This is becoming a real necessity. If established they could give an incentive to more writers in our country's languages. This is more so for languages whose orthographies have been standardized by the Indigenous Languages Unit of the Ministry of Education and the University. The languages with standardized orthographies so far are Mende, Temne, Limba, Krio, Kono and Sherbro.

As in many other educational, cultural and social affairs in life, publishing in our own languages in the developing Third World must present us with problems. However, if we stop seeing our Third World heritage as third best, and if a determined effort and sacrifice are made on all fronts, success will be ours. If as the late Mr Currey, the famous cocoa and coffee peddler, put it, we realize our own and we patronize our own, the world will not only realize but also appreciate our own Krio productions as being as good as any other writing.

Finally, writing, composing and appreciating works in Krio and other Sierra Leone mother tongues will not only contribute to our educational values but also to our social and cultural awakening and development.

References

Calendar, E. (ed.), 1985, *Krio Songs*. Freetown: People's Educational Association of Sierra Leone.

Coomber, M.E.A. & Turay, A.K. (eds.), 1981, *A Krio-Orthography Workshop*. Freetown: Ministry of Education.

Coomber, M.E.A. (ed.), 1984, *Mi Fɔs Ridin Buk* (*My First Reading Book—Books 1 & 2*). Freetown: Department of Education.

Dalby, D., 1980, *Draft Recommendation to the Sierra Leone Ministry of Education on the Use of National Languages in Education*. London: Ministry of Education and Science.

During, C. (ed.), 1986, *Kapu Sɛns Nɔ Kapu Wɔd* (*Krio Stories*). Freetown: People's Educational Association of Sierra Leone.

Fitzjohn, J. (ed.), 1986, *Kɔmɔjade*. Freetown: Sierra Leone Association of Writers and Illustrators (SLAWI).

Fyle, C.N., 1975, "A National Language Policy and the Teacher of English in Sierra Leone", *Journal of Education*, Vol. 10:2.

Fyle, C.N. and Jones, E.D., 1980, *A Krio English Dictionary*. Oxford and Freetown: Oxford University Press and Sierra Leone University Press.

Lutheran Bible Translators Inc., 1985, *Gud Yus Fɔ ɔlman: Di Nyu Testament*. United Bible Societies.

KARL I. SANDRED and NEVILLE SHRIMPTON

The Uppsala-Umeå-Freetown Krio Research and Publications Project

Introduction

In the field of English language studies William Labov's investigation of the speech of the Lower East Side of New York City (1966) marked the beginning of lively research into aspects of language in society. In a recent article, Manfred Görlach (1989) draws attention to a later publication of similar importance, Josua Fishman's book, *The Spread of English: The Sociology of English as an Additional Language* (1977), which reflected the interest arising from the increasing international use of English as well as the linguistic problems encountered in post-colonial anglophone states. However, this work has not had the same effect. There is still a lack of adequate investigations in this field, because many of these matters have not yet been taken seriously by linguists. When there have been problems in individual countries, they have usually been solved on a pragmatic level without the assistance of professional language planning.

Although there is a lack of investigations, various labels have been devised to serve as brief descriptions of the position of English in different countries. Besides being a native language in many parts of the world (ENL), English is taught all over the world as a foreign language (EFL). Societies in which English is used as a second language (ESL) are of particular sociolinguistic interest. This is commented on by Görlach (1989). In such cases English may be used in the country's administration, in the media and perhaps in the schools and universities, in addition to one or several native languages. In some countries where Standard English is the prestige language, people may normally use another variety of English in their private conversations. This is the situation, for instance, in Scotland, where the Scots have long had their own variety of northern English, Lowland Scots, as a medium of everyday communication, although Standard English is the official language (ESD). This has sometimes been described as a case of *diglossia*, but Trudgill (1974: 116 ff.) has raised objections to such a use of this term, which normally assigns for the two varieties specialised social functions which do not really apply in Scotland (cf. Sandred 1983:21). That Lowland Scots does not qualify as more than a dialect has been made clear by Aitken (1981: 72).

The recent British television series *The Story of English*, which has been shown in the US and in Britain and which has also been used in teaching in several countries, provided telling evidence of the widespread interest in the rise of English as a world language. It was accompanied by a popular handbook by Robert McCrum *et al.* This series presents varieties of English which occur throughout the world and also languages which derive, at least partly, from English, but which have changed so radically in the process that they have to be seen as distinct language systems, as in the case of Krio, which is presented in one of the episodes in which Professor Eldred Jones himself is interviewed.

Although many objections have been raised both to the book and the programmes, called by one critic "an exercise in popularisation", there is no denying that this series was a great success and created an interest in the history of English among new groups of people. Thanks to the modern medium of television, knowledge about the English language was spread more widely than had ever been possible earlier. Because of the socio-historical approach and the historical explanations given, it also taught people to look with more understanding and tolerance at varieties of English and languages which were once referred to as daughters of English, whatever their origins.

ENL, EFL, etc. Classifications not Absolute

The classification of countries as ENL, EFL, ESL, ESD, etc. nations can be misleading if they are taken to be absolute. Görlach points out that the distances between the two Englishes in an ESL or ESD country can be so great that the situation is more or less that of an EFL country. Many countries, moreover, are mixed, because they consist of subcommunities of, for instance, ENL, ESD, ESL speakers. A country's ESL status may change, for example, if a national language is promoted to replace English, when it becomes an EFL country.

It has proved difficult to apply the basic assumptions on which sociolinguistic investigations like Labov's of American urban societies were based to English in other parts of the world. Already in investigations of some European urban communities researchers had found that the idea of a "speech community" broke down. A number of articles in a volume edited by Susanne Romaine (*Sociolinguistic Variation in Speech Communities*, 1982) illustrate, in the editor's words, "the problems encountered in applying Labovian models in what are essentially a range of more linguistically diverse Old World communities". In my own investigation of attitudes to lexical and grammatical usages in Edinburgh, I found that the idea of Edinburgh as a "speech community" in Gumperz's sense cannot be sustained. In a great number of cases many informants were totally unaware of the linguistic norms (Sandred 1983 and 1985). In his studies of creole continua, Bickerton found that intuitions about grammaticality and acceptability are wholly uninterpretable. "The investigator who relies solely on intuitional evidence is thus placed in an impossible position" (Bickerton 1975: 201 f.). So the concept of a "speech community" becomes almost useless in multilingual situations, and the same applies to the concept of "competence", even if it is extended to include communicative competence, as Görlach notes. He adds that linguistic description by means of statistical methods in such situations also encounters fundamental problems.

Speaking about areas that have been overlooked by sociolinguistic researchers Görlach quotes Daswani (1978), who complains that Indian English has only been described as a list of details (deviances, additions, losses and gaps). This cannot be considered a proper description for such a description must include the geographical as well as the social distribution of the phenomena and answer questions such as: Which speakers of English in India can be regarded as speakers of Indian English? Görlach says that the lack of sociolinguistic studies of second-language-user communities is conspicuous, and there is widespread uncertainty as to how such projects could be carried out.

To illustrate what we may find along the paths of research into these areas Görlach quotes some results by Platt from studies of English used in Singapore, which show that, for an educated speaker of English in Singapore, communicative competence demands a range that also includes parts of the mesolect for informal uses.

Krio Research and Publications Project

The idea for a Krio language and literature project in Sweden was first conceived in the years 1979—80 when Karl I. Sandred, Neville Shrimpton and Sulayman Njie were all attached to the University of Umeå in northern Sweden. There happened to be several Krio-speaking students at Umeå at the time, and we started recording them, at first simply because we needed material for a university course called "Global English" which was given in the English Department. Our interest in Krio grew rapidly, partly since, like other creole studies, the study of Krio is clearly of great importance for the study of historical linguistic variation and social linguistics in general.

Because the present generation of Swedish "anglicists" was greatly influenced by the ideas of Noam Chomsky (and there is no denying their great importance in the history of linguistic research), the emphasis among researchers in English departments in Sweden has been laid on the study of standard forms of modern English. There has been a movement away not only from more traditional areas where Sweden has long had a strong position internationally, such as language history, dialectology and onomastics, but the new interest in sociolinguistics which has led to renewal of research into dialectal variation, urban dialects and contact linguistics has also taken a back seat until recently. While it would be true to say that linguistic variation has been a central field of research in English departments in Sweden, this research has mostly been based on computer-based materials which contain, almost exclusively, examples of educated Standard English for the most widely documented varieties, i.e. corpora such as the Brown Corpus (for American English), the Lancaster-Oslo/Bergen Corpus (for British English) and the London-Lund Corpus (for spoken English). These computer-based materials contain, almost without exception, examples of educated Standard English for the most widely documented varieties.

That the situation in Sweden was not without parallels internationally may be seen from the following quotation from Professor Sture Ureland in the Department of General Linguistics at the University of Mannheim. He writes, "The place for contact perspectives in theoretical linguistics for describing language change was even more constrained during the dominance of the generative school in the 1960s and 1970s, which delimited the scope of linguistic research to a monolingual and monolectal speaker . . . The goal of such studies was mostly standardised varieties of the major national languages" (Ureland 1989: 245).

It quickly became evident that limited materials such as the recordings we were making at that time would not be sufficient for an extended research project for the study of Krio. What we were aiming at was in fact a project in contact linguistics. The proper materials were only available in the countries where the language was spoken. We had already corresponded with Professor Eldred Jones, co-author of the *Krio-English Dictionary*, published by Oxford University Press in 1980. At a meeting in Sweden and during visits to Freetown by Neville Shrimpton some preliminary co-operation with Sierra Leone researchers, educationalists and Krio dramatists was outlined and initiated. Needless to say, a project like ours would not have been possible without external economic support. This was obtained from the Swedish Agency for Research Cooperation with Developing Countries (SAREC). Since the assembling of material from which other researchers and educationalists can also benefit must be important in our project, we founded a *Krio Publications Series*, in which we have now completed the publication of six Krio dramas.

The theme of the workshop that has been organised here is not the theoretical foundations of research into various language varieties and systems but the practical applications of the fact that West Africa is an area where English is

A pupil reading Krio sentences from the blackboard in a pilot-project class (Photograph Neville Shrimpton).

both a native language and a second language. In one form or another it is the mother tongue of a great number of people. The language system which we are concerned with is the one called West African Krio. Originally only a spoken language, the days when Krio was not considered fit for written uses are long since gone, and today it is no longer solely an oral language but can rightly claim to be a medium of a culture and literature which deserves the same respect as any other language and its culture. John Spencer expressed a generally accepted opinion among modern linguists in an article entitled "Language and Development in Africa" when he wrote that all languages have "an equal capacity to expand their resources in order to accommodate to the developing communicative needs of their community" (Spencer 1985: 390). The potential of Krio as a literary medium has been demonstrated by a number of authors who have had the courage to write, for instance, poetry and drama in Krio, and Thomas Decker showed how well even a classic English author such as Shakespeare can be rendered in Krio. It is a source of satisfaction that we have had the opportunity in Sweden of publishing a few of these works in our *Krio Publications Series*.

We are very grateful to the authors and other people who have made this workshop possible, after the necessary funding had been obtained from

SAREC. Our thanks are also due to Professor Eldred Jones who has been our chief advisor in editorial matters and to Mr Ajayi Coomber for invaluable help with regard to questions connected with the new orthography. In addition to literary texts we now also hope to be able to publish folklore material, i.e. Krio folk traditions, fables and tales, and articles by people working with and writing in Krio in Sierra Leone. Here I am thinking particularly of all those who are using it in teaching, health campaigns and the media. I shall not at this point go into the difficulties we have had in finding funds for the cost of publication. The printing has been done at Umeå University, which gave some support at the initial stage. The Swedish Council for Research in the Humanities and Social Sciences (HSFR) has supported the publication of volumes four to six. The future, however, is very uncertain.

The Production and Publication of Krio Texts

To date, six editions of the *Krio Publications Series* (Shrimpton and Njie 1982—) have been produced, albeit at a somewhat sporadic rate. When preparing these editions for publication we were faced with a number of important decisions concerning our general policy for the series. Not least amongst these was, of course, the question of orthography, one of the main themes of this workshop. Three editions of the series came out between the years 1982 and 1984. Our work on these was thus started after the publication of the *Krio-English Dictionary* (Fyle and Jones 1980) with its clear guidelines for spelling the language. It was also at this time that various groups were meeting at orthography workshops to finalise suggestions for the standard orthographies of a number of the indigenous languages of Sierra Leone, including Krio (Sierra Leone Ministry of Education, *a, b, c, d* and *e*). Our situation was difficult; we were in contact with Professor Eldred Jones and we knew that it was reasonably certain that the future standard orthography would be determined by these workshops and by the recommendations outlined and used in the *Dictionary*. On the other hand, we were also in contact with authors who were writing in Krio, and it very soon became evident that many of them were not yet in favour of adopting these recommendations. The reasons for this were somewhat complicated. To a certain extent, it seemed that there was some antagonism between town and gown—the writers and the University (Fourah Bay College). At that time few, if any, of the authors with whom we spoke had any connection with the University. Some of them maintained that the *Dictionary* recommendations were too academic; the *Dictionary* itself was certainly too expensive, as Professor Jones himself has pointed out, and this may have done a lot to make people feel that it, and its orthography, were not for the man in the street. There were other reasons as well. Many of the writers concerned had known, and even worked with, the dramatist Thomas Decker. They knew his orthography (as used in Decker *b*) and sometimes used his recommendations when they wrote their plays. For them the great advantage of his spelling system was that it did not make use of 'phonetic' letters like ɔ, ɛ, and ŋ.

As outsiders, we felt that we should not pre-empt any official decision with regard to the orthography. We considered that it simply was not our business to promote one orthography rather than another, particularly if that meant coercing authors into doing something which was against their better judgement. One of our main aims in producing the *Krio Publications Series* was to help Krio authors and to provide them with copies of their plays, not to convert them to a particular spelling system. We had stated our own opinions on the sort of orthography that we preferred elsewhere (Shrimpton 1982)— namely that we basically favoured the Fyle-Jones recommendations. As a result of this policy decision, then, we left the actual choice of the orthography to the individual writers.

Our task seemed clear. We would assemble texts, make a choice between them, regularise the orthographies within their own frameworks, introduce the author, provide background information about the plays, the literary scene, the language itself and problems of orthography, etc. This seemed straightforward enough. In actual fact, the process of editing the texts was to prove far more time-consuming and far more difficult than we could possibly have imagined at the outset. This was not only because the texts varied so much with regard to spelling; it was also because the manuscripts often reached us in such varying conditions from other points of view as well. Many that we have received or 'collected' on the spot (our main method) are rough acting copies that may be easy enough to deal with and adjust at rehearsals, say, but which are harder to decipher and alter when the author is not on hand to ask about details or inconsistencies. Even when the text itself has been fully interpreted, and final problems discussed with the author, there remain other difficulties for which there have not always been clear solutions or external guidelines. This is particularly true of such questions as word boundaries (i.e. where to divide up words, whether to use hyphens and similar problems). We are very doubtful about the use of hyphens at all except in exceptional cases; one of the few possible instances where it seems appropriate or at least defensible is in the case of compound surnames, for instance Lunge-Jɔnsin. Even the question of punctuation is a vexed one. It is not enough merely to say that one can apply the same criteria as for English punctuation. On the whole, however, things have gradually become easier as our contact and collaboration with people who are directly involved with these types of questions here in Sierra Leone has increased.

The first edition in the series was Mr. Dele Charley's *Petikot Kohna*, for which Thomas Decker's orthography was used. In the case of the next volume in the series, Mr. Charley's *Fatmata*, we printed the text in both Decker's orthography and in that of Fyle and Jones in order to give people some idea of the alternatives that were available. Volume 3, Mrs. Esther Taylor Pearce's *Queen Esther*, on the other hand, was printed in her own non-phonemic orthography. As was pointed out in another paper at this workshop, we have used the term 'mixed' for this type of orthography. In fact, it is a good example of the sort of orthography that many people still use when they write Krio. It could even be called a 'natural' orthography, as orthographies of this type have actually developed in various, generally unorganised ways, out of earlier attempts to write Krio. In this respect, such orthographies mirror the sort of development that took place in the case of English (see, for example, Scragg 1974) and many other 'established' languages. Whereas the orthography of Fyle and Jones, like that of Thomas Decker, aims at regularity, with one letter or one combination of letters representing one phoneme or cluster of phonemes, mixed orthographies are distinguished by a lack of regularity. In the case of a mixed Krio orthography many of the words will be written exactly as they are in English, and where this is not the case, those regularities which are introduced will be governed more by English spelling conventions than by general phonetic principles. Compare the various representations below of three lines from Thomas Decker's translation into Krio of Shakespeare's *Julius Caesar*[1]—first in his regularised orthography, then in a mixed orthography, and finally in the new standard orthography:

> *Antoni.* Padi dem, kohntri, una ohl wey dey
> Na Rom. Meyk una kak una yeys ya.
> A kam ber Siza, a noh kam preys am.

> *Antony.* Paddy dem, country, una all way day
> Nar Rome. Make una all kack una yase yar.
> Are cam berr Caesar, are nor cam praise am.

> *Antoni.* Padi dɛm, kɔntri, una ɔl we de
> Na Rom. Mek una kak una yes ya.
> A kam bɛr Siza, a nɔ kam pres am.

When we came to publish the next three volumes in the series (1988), more general agreement had been reached about the question of a standard orthography. Partly, there was less opposition, on the whole, to the recommendations of Fyle and Jones or to those of the orthography workshops,[2] but

---

[1] *Antony.* "Friends, Romans, countrymen, lend me your ears. I come to bury Caesar, not to praise him." (*Julius Caesar*, Act III, Scene II)

[2] The recommendations arrived at by the orthography workshop groups were essentially the same as those of Fyle and Jones. The former did, however, add the letter ŋ and they also for-

also people seemed to have come to realise that it was important to settle on one orthography which could be promoted in education and elsewhere. Now that there was a clear 'official' system of spelling, and authors were more disposed to accept it, we decided to recommend those writers whose works we published in our series to adopt it and to let us transpose their texts into it. We did make one last exception in the case of Thomas Decker's *Juliohs Siza* (Volume 4). Following the wishes of his family we used his orthography. It would have seemed wrong not to, considering the battles that he had waged on behalf of the Krio language and the fact that *Juliohs Siza*, and the orthography in which he wrote his final version of it, represented the culmination of his career as a Krio writer. For Volumes 5 and 6, however, we used the new standard orthography, and were greatly helped with this by Mr. Ajayi Coomber at Fourah Bay College.

By the time we produced Volumes 4—6 we had transferred our texts to a computer and begun to build up a small Krio database. We had started doing this on an IBM system but soon found that it was more practical and cheaper to go over to Macintosh computers. This was largely because it was so much easier to create and print the new letters in the standard alphabet, namely ɔ, ɛ and ŋ, using Macintoshes. Initially, the main purpose of the database was to make it easier for us to edit texts in the Krio series, but we also saw that once texts were available in such a way they would automatically form a corpus of language material which could be used for linguistic research—in particular, for an analysis of the grammar of Krio and for the compiling of Krio dictionaries. We used two basic and very cheap font editors called *Fontastic* and *Fontographer*[3] for creating the three letters we needed. Since we were working with a Swedish keyboard, we incorporated these by programming the keys for the Swedish letters *å, ä* and *ö* to produce ɔ, ɛ and ŋ instead. Apart from the ease with which we could now create the new letters, there were many other advantages in using a computer. For the actual word-processing we used the *Microsoft Word* programme. *Word* contains a spelling-check which also allows you to build up your own spelling-checks. As we have transferred texts to the database we have been able to construct our own Krio spelling-check and to use it for each new text we edit. The basic word-search facilities in *Word* can also be used for finding language items that are needed for analysis. Our current aim is to develop programmes on the Macintosh that would make it possible for us to ask the machine to give us a list of, for example, all the occurrences of a particular word or grammatical

---

mulated, in some cases, more explicit recommendations with regard to such matters as punctuation and word division.

[3] Produced by Altsys Corporation, 720 Avenue F, Suite 108, Plano. Texas 75074, USA.

feature in the Krio corpus, together with all the contexts in which it occurs. At present we can only do this on the IBM system.[4]

To aid us in our linguistic analysis of the language material we have enlisted the help of undergraduate and postgraduate students in the Department of English at Umeå University. These students have chosen to write their course dissertations on topics connected with Krio grammar and lexis, and they have used the texts in the series as their material. Most of the work that has been done so far has been on the verb phrase. In particular, we have been looking at tense and aspect. We have been concerned with testing various suggestions about the ways in which Krio verbs indicate completion, habit, time relationships, etc. For instance, we have been able to confirm earlier suggestions that the basic division of verbs into statives and non-statives is crucial for an understanding of how the Krio verb system works.[5] We have been concerned with an investigation of areas such as: the distinction between statives and non-statives with regard to past-time reference; habitual, iterative, continuative (progressive) and completive aspect and the use in this respect of the pre-verbal markers *de, kin, kin de* and *dɔn*; the future (irrealis) marker *go* and a comparison between the use of this marker, the use of the stem form and the use of *de* to express future time; redundancy with particular reference to the marking of plurality and to the use or non-use of the definite and indefinite articles; the influence of English on Krio and the whole question of decreolisation and Krio-English language contact. We are at present in the process of preparing a report on this work and this will be made available to all who are interested.

The transfer of the texts to a database also enables us to produce editions in the series in Braille. This has involved us in a number of new difficulties, most of which we have been able to overcome with the help of Professor Eldred Jones, technical assistance from Mr. Åke Sandgren at Umeå University and advice from the National Institute for the Blind in London. At present Braille versions of Volumes 4—6 can be ordered from us, as can the text of Thomas Decker's adaptation of Shakespeare's *As You Like It*, which he called *Udat di Kiap Fit* (Decker c). These are in the new standard orthography, and, luckily, the new letters did not cause any serious problems here, as there were already international recommendations for their Braille counterparts.

We now hope to be able to continue the work we have started and also to continue the close collaboration we have had with our colleagues in Freetown.

---

[4] Since this paper was given, a new programme for creating such concordances on the Macintosh has been announced. It will be available in 1991 from the Department of Russian and Slavic Studies at McGill University in Montreal, Canada.

[5] Cf. on this, with references to Bickerton, Romaine 1988: 175 f.

Our aims are far from being only academic. We hope that the results of our research will help to provide a basis for the production of materials which will be of practical use in education and in the dissemination of literature in Krio. Our work on the grammar and lexis of the language has already begun to give us new insights into phenomena which are of relevance for general linguistic theory, and we are happy to have been able to introduce students and colleagues in Sweden to a fascinating area of study. In a wider perspective our hope is that we shall be able to make a contribution to the spread of knowledge about Krio culture and the linguistic and literary expressions of this culture. Ultimately, we would like to feel that we had also contributed to the spread of Krio literacy.

Bibliography

Aitken, A.J., 1981, "The Good Old Scots Tongue: Does Scots have an Identity?", *Minority Languages Today*, eds. E. Haugen, J.D. McClure and D.S. Thomson, Edinburgh: Edinburgh University Press, 72—90.

Bickerton, D., 1975, *Dynamics of a Creole System*. New York: Cambridge University Press.

Daswani, C.J., 1978, "Some Theoretical Implications for Investigating Indian English", *Indian Writing in English*, ed. M. Ramesh. New Delhi: Orient Longman, 115—128.

Decker, T., *a* (no date, published in 1964), *Julius Caesar* (mixed-orthography version). Freetown: Privately mimeographed edition.

— *b* (no date, published in 1965), *Julius Caesar* (Decker's regularised-orthography version). Freetown: Privately mimeographed edition.

— *c* (no date). *Udat di Kiap Fit*. Freetown: Privately mimeographed edition.

Fishman, J.A., *et al.*, 1977, *The Spread of English. The Sociology of English as an Additional Language*. Rowley Mass: Newbury House.

Fyle, C.N., and Jones, E.D., 1980, *A Krio-English Dictionary*. Oxford and Freetown: Oxford University Press and Sierra Leone University Press.

Görlach, M., 1989, "The Sociolinguistics of English as a World Language", *Critical Approaches to the New Literatures in English*, A Selection of Papers of the 10th Annual Conference on 'Commonewalth' Literature and Language Studies, Koenigstein, 11—14 June, 1987, ed. D. Riemenschneider. Essen: Die Blaue Eule, 116—130.

Gumperz, J., 1968, "The Speech Community", reprinted in 1972 in *Language and Social Context*, ed. P.P. Giglioli. Hammondsworth: Penguin Education, 219—231.

Jones, E.D., see Fyle, C.N., and Jones, E.D.

Labov, W., 1966, *The Social Stratification of English in New York City*. Washington D.C.: Center for Applied Linguistics.

McCrum, R., Cran, W., and MacNeal, R., 1986, *The Story of English*. New York: Elisabeth Sifton Books. Viking.

Platt, J., Weber, H., and Ho, M.L., 1983, *Singapore and Malaysia* (Varieties of English around the World T4). Amsterdam: John Benjamins.

Romaine, S., (ed.), 1982, *Sociolinguistic Variation in Speech Communities*. London: Edward Arnold.

— 1988, *Pidgin and Creole Languages*. London and New York: Longman.

Sandred, K.I., 1983, *Good or Bad Scots? Attitudes to Optional Lexical and Grammatical Usages in Edinburgh* (Studia Anglistica Upsaliensia 48). Stockholm: Almqvist & Wiksell International.

— 1985, "Overt and Covert Prestige: Evaluative Boundaries in the Speech Community", *Focus on Scotland* (Varieties of English around the World G5). Amsterdam: John Benjamins, 69—86.

Scragg, D.G., 1974, *A History of English Spelling*. Manchester: Manchester University Press.

Shrimpton, N., 1982, "Au (Aw?) fo (foh?) rayt (rait? write?) Krio?", *West Africa*, 1 March 1982, 561—563.

Shrimpton, N. and Njie, S. (eds.), 1982, *Krio Publications Series*. Umeå: Umeå University. 1. Dele Charley, *Petikot Kohna*, 1982. 2. Dele Charley, *Fatmata*, 1983. 3. Esther Taylor-Pearce, *Queen Esther*, 1984. 4. Thomas Decker, *Juliohs Siza*, 1988. 5. Lawrence Quaku-Woode, *Gɔd Pas Kɔnsibul*, 1988. 6. Esther Taylor-Pearce, *Bad Man Bɛtɛ Pas ɛmti Os*, 1989.

Sierra Leone Ministry of Education, *a* (no date), *A Mende Orthography Workshop* (workshop held January 21—25, 1980). Freetown: Ministry of Education.

— *b* (no date), *A Themne Orthography Workshop* (workshop held February 18—22, 1980). Freetown: Ministry of Education.

— *c* (no date), *A Krio Orthography Workshop* (workshop held November 24—25, 1981). Freetown: Ministry of Education.

— *d* (no date), *Report of the Writers' Workshop of the Indigenous Languages Education Project* (workshop held April 3—9, 1983). Freetown: Ministry of Education.

— *e* (no date), *Revised Kono, Krio, Limba, Mende and Themne Orthographies* (workshop held April 24—27, 1984). Freetown: Ministry of Education.

Spencer, J., 1985, "Language and Development in Africa: The Unequal Equation", *Language of Inequality*, ed. Nessa Wolfson and Joan Manes (Contributions to the Sociology of Language 36), Berlin, New York, Amsterdam: Mouton Publishers, 387—397.

Thomason, Sarah Grey, and Kaufman, T., 1988, *Language Contact, Creolisation, and Genetic Linguistics*. Berkeley and Los Angeles: University of California Press.

Trudgill, P., 1974, *Sociolinguistics. An Introduction*. Harmondsworth: Penguin.

Ureland, S., 1989, "Some Contact Structures in Scandinavian, Dutch and Raeto-Romansh. Inner-Linguistic and/or Contact Causes of Language Change", *Language Change. Contributions to the Study of its Causes*, ed. L.E. Breivik and E.H. Jahr. Berlin: Mouton de Gruyter, 239—276.

REPUBLIC OF SIERRA LEONE

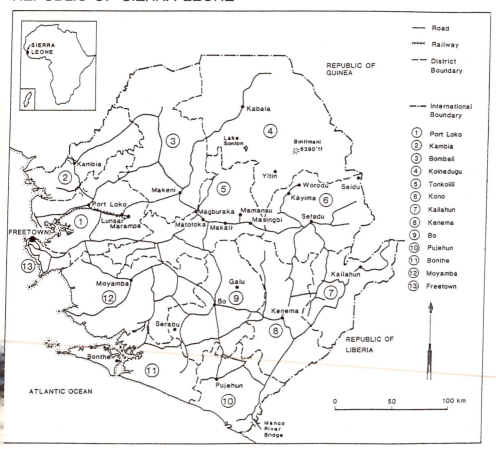